THE COMPLETE CARDINAL GUIDE

TO PLANNING FOR AND LIVING IN

RETIREMENT

WORKBOOK

NAVIGATING SOCIAL SECURITY,
MEDICARE AND SUPPLEMENTAL INSURANCE,
LONG-TERM CARE, IRA, LIFE INSURANCE,
POST-RETIREMENT INVESTMENT AND INCOME TAXES

Cardinal, an adjective—"of the greatest importance; fundamental"
Synonyms: fundamental, basic, main, chief, primary, crucial, pivotal, prime, principal, paramount, preeminent, highest, key, essential.

- When do I start my Social Security check?
- How do I supplement Medicare?
- Should I purchase Long-Term Care Insurance?
- What should I do with my IRA or 401(k)?
- Am I investing to have enough income in retirement?
- How do I plan for income taxes after age 65?
- How do I handle life insurance and transferring assets to children and grandchildren?
- How do I choose financial and legal professionals to help me?

THE COMPLETE CARDINAL GUIDE TO PLANNING FOR AND LIVING IN RETIREMENT WORKBOOK

NAVIGATING SOCIAL SECURITY,
MEDICARE AND SUPPLEMENTAL INSURANCE,
LONG-TERM CARE, IRA, LIFE INSURANCE,
POST-RETIREMENT INVESTMENT AND INCOME TAXES

Hans Scheil
Douglas Amis

Leapfolio

A joint-venture partner of Tupelo Press
North Adams, Massachusetts

CONTENTS

INTRODUCTION

In 2016, we at Cardinal published our *Complete Cardinal Guide to Planning for and Living in Retirement*. We've been in the retirement planning business for more than 40 years, and people still come to us, day in and day out, with the same kinds of basic questions about how to navigate this complex and critically important activity. We wanted to write a book that would provide an overview of the major problems that retirees face and the simple strategies you can implement now, with the help of professionals, to make your retirement financially successful. We wanted this book to be useful to people in their 70s and 80s who are living through the difficulties retirees face. It's challenging to manage the details of Social Security, Medicare, long-term care, life insurance, IRAs, investment assets, and paying taxes. We wrote the *Complete Cardinal Guide* to help.

The *Guide* has fulfilled our expectations and proved to be a success. In the past year, we've sold or distributed to our clients more than 6,000 copies. And we've gotten positive feedback that people find the book to be a useful introduction to these complicated topics. But we've also learned that the *Guide* isn't quite sufficient by itself. So we've created this *Workbook* to accompany it. In the *Workbook*, we provide additional detailed examples of real-life situations, products, and strategies, as well as guidance to help you prepare to discuss your retirement planning with a professional advisor. The *Workbook* is organized into modules that correspond with the chapters in the *Guide*, in the same order. (Note, however, that because the *Guide* begins with a chapter telling Hans' personal and family story, Module 1 goes with Chapter 2, Module 2 goes with Chapter 3, etc.). You may find this *Workbook* valuable by itself, but we recommend that you use it in conjunction with the *Guide*.

As we say throughout *The Complete Cardinal Guide to Planning for and Living in Retirement*: **It's never too late to begin sound retirement planning, and it's always a good idea to consult with professionals.** And the sooner you begin, the more likely it is that you'll be able to avoid having to make important but challenging decisions in the midst of a crisis. We look forward to serving you.

Hans Scheil
Doug Amis

| **SOCIAL SECURITY**

KEY QUESTIONS

- When can I start to receive Social Security retirement benefits?

- How does my spouse receiving a Social Security benefit affect me?

- What happens when my spouse dies if we were both receiving Social Security?

- How does Social Security help me pay for long-term care?

- Who should I consult for advice in making decisions about my Social Security benefits?

Corresponds to Chapter 2, "Strategizing Your Social Security Benefits,"
*in **The Complete Cardinal Guide.***

1.1 A Bit of History

Social Security began as a response to the challenging economic head winds the United States faced following the Great War, the Great Depression, and the failure of company pensions. President Franklin D. Roosevelt routinely received requests for assistance. One letter, from Mrs. M. A. Zoller on behalf of her 82-year-old mother who had no means of support, included a news clipping advocating a national pension paying $1.00 per day for people over 60 years old. This proposed national program would be similar to the various old age pension laws already established by 25 state legislatures. The Old Age, Survivors, and Disability Insurance program was put into effect with the passage of the Social Security Act in 1935. What we call Social Security today is a combination of several different programs that together pay retirement and disability payments to millions of Americans, including children's benefits and survivors' benefits. Altogether, Social Security is one of the largest expenditures by the federal government.

Social Security, in its current state, allows retirees to choose to receive their Social Security benefits as early as age 62. **People who opt to start Social Security at 62 receive a reduced benefit. Your full benefit is payable only if you retire at Full Retirement Age.** *Full Retirement Age* **(FRA) is based on your birth year.** Today most retirees have a Full Retirement Age of 66 (birth year 1943 to 1954). For retirees born after 1954 the FRA will gradually increase to age 67.

You can also choose to delay your Social Security benefits. You can earn deferred retirement credits by delaying your benefits past your Full Retirement Age. Benefits increase for every month you delay past FRA up to age 70. The increase is about 8% for every 12 months of delay. The average retirement benefit paid to a Social Security beneficiary is $1,302.86 per month (2016).

The first steps to decide if you are ready to start your journey onto Social Security involve confirming eligibility and finding the primary insurance amount for you and your family. But before we do that, let's spend a few minutes understanding the math behind Social Security and the different factors that will affect your retirement benefits.

Reading Check

At what age can a person start receiving their Social Security benefits? When does a person become eligible for Full Retirement benefits? How long can a person delay drawing their Social Security?

1.2 Earning Social Security Credits

Prior to 1978, the path to becoming fully insured by Social Security was very different than the way it is done today. Employers would report quarterly earnings for their employees: Earning $50 in a three-month period would earn a worker a credit. Forty credits is the maximum that means one is fully insured by Social Security, so it used to take 10 years of work to reach that level. Since 1978, however, employers report earnings only once a year, and credits are based on a person's earnings. As of our date of publication, $1,260 of covered earnings in a year will earn a worker one Social Security credit. $5,040 of covered earnings will earn a worker four Social Security Credits, the maximum for any one year. (The earnings figure can change from year to year.)

Keep in mind, only income that is subject to the Social Security tax counts toward your Social Security earnings. Sources of income like dividends on investments and interest on savings do not count toward Social Security. Due to the change in rules, you could earn enough in one quarter to earn one year's worth of credits. If you have a high-paying job you could earn your 40 credits over 10 years with only 30 months of actual work instead of 120.

Reading Check

After coming home late from his lodge meeting, Bernie notices his wife, Ethel, sifting through a stack of papers, deep in thought, tapping a pencil on a notepad. When Bernie asks Ethel what she is doing, she says she wants to make sure they both have enough credits to start receiving full Social Security retirement benefits. Unsure of the answer, Bernie gives you a call to see if you know anything about Social Security credits, since you have recently started collecting your Social Security. What would you tell Bernie and Ethel?

1.3 Determining Full Retirement Age

Many of the people retiring today are eligible to receive their full retirement benefits at age 66. But it's different for people born after 1954. Use the chart below to confirm your Full Retirement Age, based on your year of birth.

Fig. 1.1

Year of Birth*	Full Retirement Age
1937 or earlier	65
1938	65 and 2 months
1939	65 and 4 months
1940	65 and 6 months
1941	65 and 8 months
1942	65 and 10 months
1943–1954	66
1955	66 and 2 months
1956	66 and 4 months
1957	66 and 6 months
1958	66 and 8 months
1959	66 and 10 months
1960 and later	67

If you were born on January 1, you should base your FRA on the previous year.

Full Retirement Age is part of the formula used to determine your retirement benefit. However, your FRA is not necessarily the optimal time for you to elect your benefit. Choosing when to start your benefit is a personal decision. The economic impact of Social Security on the average retiree's household is remarkable: The average individual lifetime benefit from Social Security is more than $300,000. It is especially important for couples to understand the impact of Social Security planning to ensure that if one spouse dies, the surviving spouse has enough income.

Reading Check

Use the chart above to determine the Full Retirement age of Betty and Sue in the following example:

Betty and Sue are two sisters who are planning to retire soon. After discussions with their retirement planner and Certified Financial Planner™ professional, they both realize that figuring out their Full Retirement Age is the first step in determining their possible Social Security benefits. Betty was born on November 1, 1954. Sue was born four years later on June 15, 1958. At what age does Betty reach her Full Retirement Age? When does Sue reach her FRA?

1.4 Estimating Retirement Benefits

The Social Security program bases your monthly retirement benefit on your lifetime earnings history. To determine this information, the Social Security Administration (SSA) performs a series of calculations. These calculations include adjusting or indexing your actual earnings to account for changes in average wages since the year they were earned. The SSA uses data from at least 35 years (picking your highest-earning years and using $0 for any years missing earnings data). All of this data is used to determine your monthly retirement benefit, or Primary Insurance Amount (PIA).

You don't need to do the research to understand how the SSA arrived at your personal Primary Insurance Amount. There is a much easier way to find your PIA: You can request a Social Security Earnings Report online, or in print.

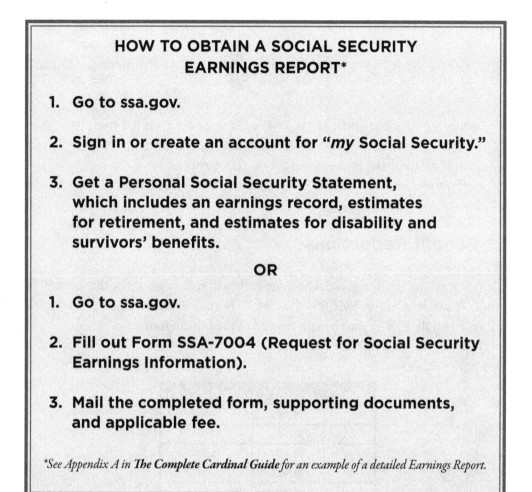

HOW TO OBTAIN A SOCIAL SECURITY EARNINGS REPORT*

1. **Go to ssa.gov.**

2. **Sign in or create an account for *"my* Social Security."**

3. **Get a Personal Social Security Statement, which includes an earnings record, estimates for retirement, and estimates for disability and survivors' benefits.**

OR

1. **Go to ssa.gov.**

2. **Fill out Form SSA-7004 (Request for Social Security Earnings Information).**

3. **Mail the completed form, supporting documents, and applicable fee.**

See Appendix A in **The Complete Cardinal Guide for an example of a detailed Earnings Report.*

High earners may find that only a portion of their income has been taxed for Social Security purposes over the years. This inherently limits the amount that Social Security will pay out. If you have earned above the Social Security taxation limit for 35 years you will receive the Maximum Benefit. This limit grows from year to year with inflation or by legislation. For 2016, the maximum amount of taxable earnings is $118,500. **The *Maximum Benefit* is the highest amount of money that Social Security will pay a person, and that number is based on the amount of taxes they paid in to Social Security.**

Reading Check

What is the easiest way to learn how much your Social Security check will be?

———•———

While attending a baseball game with your friend Alfred, he mentions that he is helping his nephew, Bruce, to estimate his retirement benefits. Alfred tells you they both have been struggling to figure out what Bruce's Primary Insurance Amount would be. What would you tell Alfred? How should Alfred and Bruce find out this information?

1.5 Benefit Reductions

Choosing to start receiving Social Security early will reduce your monthly benefit. If your Full Retirement Age is 66 but you elect to begin before you reach that age, you will receive only 75% of your benefit instead of the full amount.

Fig. 1.2 Benefit Reduction

Age	Benefit	Reduction
62	75.00%	25.00%
63	80.00%	20.00%
64	86.70%	13.30%
65	93.30%	6.70%
66	100.00%	0.00%

If you receive spousal benefits earlier than your Full Retirement Age, you will also receive a reduced amount for the rest of your life. Spousal benefits exist to compensate the lower-earning spouse who, for example, might have stayed home raising children for a number of years, thus creating a low lifetime earnings amount. The lower-earning spouse can claim benefits based upon the earnings of the higher earner.

Fig. 1.3 Spousal Benefit Reduction

Age	Benefit	Reduction
62	35.00%	15.00%
63	37.50%	12.50%
64	41.70%	8.30%
65	45.80%	4.20%
66	50.00%	0.00%

1.6 Survivor Income Planning (Early Death)

For couples, the reality that one of you may predecease the other is stark. On top of having to adjust to the distinct day-to-day changes in your life, the Social Security Administration has a different set of rules for survivors. A survivor's benefit is a payment provided to widows, widowers, and surviving divorced spouses. This monthly benefit is based on the deceased spouse's or ex-spouse's earnings history. Unlike basic Social Security retirement benefits, survivor benefits can start as early as age 60 (or as early as age 50 if the surviving spouse is disabled). Similar to starting basic Social Security benefits early, if you start survivor benefits prior to your Full Retirement Age you will be paid a reduced benefit. Waiting until your Full Retirement Age to begin receiving your survivor benefit will prevent your monthly payment from being permanently reduced.

1.7 Marriage Status and Survivor Benefits

There are some specifics you need to know if you no longer have a spouse that you were married to for at least 10 years and divorced, or if you are a surviving spouse.

Remarrying could prevent you from collecting benefits on a past spouse, depending on when you remarry.

- If you remarry before you reach age 60 (50 if disabled), you cannot receive benefits as a surviving spouse while you are married.

- If you remarry after you reach age 60 (50 if disabled), you can continue to qualify for benefits on the deceased spouse's Social Security record.

If you are a widow or widower, of any age, and care for the deceased's child who is under 16, you should be eligible to collect a survivor benefit. Different rules apply for Social Security benefits if there are minor or disabled children involved.

Divorce and survivorship present complicated scenarios. Always make sure to get personalized advice from a qualified advisor or Certified Financial Planner™ professional. Many of our clients have tried to research these situations on their own, or have copied the same decision as an older coworker. This shortcut style of planning often results in a loss of thousands of dollars and leaves them ill prepared for retirement.

1.8 Survivor Income Planning (Late Death)

You pay in to Social Security your entire working life. It is often discussed in the same context as life insurance. This leads some people to believe that when they die, the Social Security Administration will provide their loved ones with a lump-sum payout like life insurance. This is not true. There is no balance and the only death benefit Social Security offers is a one-time payment of $255. Even this small payment is subject to additional restrictions that limit who can qualify and receive it.

If you and your spouse are already receiving Social Security retirement benefits, whichever payment is larger will be paid as the survivor's benefit to the widow or widower. The lower benefit will no longer be issued. This could decrease the income of the surviving spouse by as much as 50%, while their expenses would typically decline by only 30%. Planning ahead to provide sufficient survivor income from investments, annuities, or life insurance can help prevent a financial hardship on your loved one.

In the example below, a couple's combined Social Security income is $51,660. One spouse's income is $2,971 per month, while the other's is $1,334. As illustrated in the pie graph, when one spouse dies; the lower check, $1,334 (equal to $16,008/year), will go away. It does not matter which spouse dies; the remaining spouse will get to keep the higher check. The death of the spouse creates the need to replace the $16,008 that is taken away. We've multiplied this amount by 10 and 15 to show how much income would be lost to the surviving spouse over that many years. This income would not have to be made up if a life insurance policy had been bought to automatically replace the lost income.

Fig. 1.4 Starting Household Social Security: $51,660

Plan for an after-tax amount of:	Plan for an after-tax amount of:
$160,080	$240,120
To replace lost income for:	To replace lost income for:
10 years	15 years

Survivor Social Security $35,652

Reduction $16,008

Reading Check

Roger's wife, Sarah, recently passed away. Roger has been trying to deter-mine whether or not Sarah had a remaining balance of Social Security bene-fits. He believes that he should be able to receive a large lump-sum payment. Is Roger correct in his thinking? How could Roger and Sarah have better prepared for this situation?

———•———

During your weekly dinner with your friends Myrtle and Murray, they mention that they have been preparing in case one of them passes before the other. Murray believes the survivor would get both his Social Security retirement check as well as Myrtle's. Myrtle believes that if Murray were to pass before she does, she would only keep her own Social Security check, which is small-er than Murray's. Which one of them is right?

1.9 Putting It All Together

The goal of Social Security planning is to maximize the benefit for you and your family. Using your Primary Insurance Amount and demographic data, professionals can use a maximization formula to make recommendations. The maximization process involves a fair amount of calculus (think back to optimization word problems!). Instead of bogging you down in a series of complicated calculations, let's focus on how the inputs affect the formula.

Keep in mind that any mathematical projection will only be a best guess, because it has to use assumptions like life expectancy. It is difficult to determine how long someone is going to live—no one can predict the future. Social Security maximization relies upon estimates, including your life expectancy and your Primary Insurance Amount, with the goal of finding the best path to maximizing your and your family's lifetime benefits.

Using the Life Expectancy Table below to estimate your own life expectancy will give you a good starting point. As with golf, "handicapping" the estimate by working in your own personal history can provide a better understanding of your potential life-span. If you or your family has a shorter than average life expectancy, consider reducing your estimate. Likewise, if your family has a history of longevity, then increase your estimate.

Fig. 1.5

	First to Die	Second to Die
Couple, age 55	18.6 to 23.7 years	31 to 35.6 years
Couple, age 60	15.1 to 19.6 years	26.6 to 30.9 years
Couple, age 65	12.1 to 15.8 years	22.4 to 26.2 years
Couple, age 70	9.4 to 12.3 years	18.4 to 21.8 years
Couple, age 75	7.1 to 9.2 years	14.7 to 17.6 years
Couple, age 80	5.2 to 6.7 years	11.3 to 13.8 years

Estimating your life expectancy is the key to maximizing Social Security benefits. Those who are likely to live well into their 80s will benefit from delaying their retirement benefits, but may forego income when they are younger and more active. You will need to balance the mathematical recommendation with your own needs. The mathematical process of maximization cannot account for all the nuances of your family's needs and desires.

Reading Check

If a person's family has a history of health problems, how should they project their life expectancy? How might that projection change if someone has a history of longevity in their family? Why is maximization a difficult process?

1.10 Maximizing Benefits for a Couple Age 65

In our era of continuous technological advancement, people find themselves with many more tools at their disposal. Sophisticated software once restricted to professionals is now available online for direct consumer use. These new websites help individuals acquire personalized information regarding benefit maximization. By adjusting the input variables, such as life expectancy and retirement date, you can review different potential outcomes.

In the following example, Michael and Jenny are interested in maximizing their benefits from Social Security. This is what we know about Michael and Jenny:

Male	Age 65	Good Health	Benefit @ FRA: $2,400	Life Expectancy: 87
Female	Age 65	Good Health	Benefit @ FRA: $1,200	Life Expectancy: 91

Filing at Full Retirement Age

Both Michael and Jenny are planning to retire at age 66. They can both file at age 66, get their full benefits, and would receive $43,200 in annual Social Security payments. Electing their benefit at Full Retirement Age, they would receive close to $1.411 million dollars from Social Security over the rest of their expected lifetimes. (This calculation assumes that there is a 2.39% cost-of-living adjustment each year.)

This is a considerable amount of income; to replicate these benefits, a conservative couple would need to invest $1,053,990 at 2% interest. A more aggressive couple expecting a 5% return would still need over $750,000 to reproduce the Social Security benefit shown in this example.

Optimal Filing Strategy

If Michael and Jenny can continue to work at age 66 or delay their Social Security benefits by other means, such as taxable withdrawals and using other kinds of income, they can vastly improve their Social Security income and their overall lifetime benefits.

By deferring their Social Security benefits one year, Michael and Jenny would receive an 8% increase in their monthly benefit ($2,592 and $1,296, respectively). The higher payments could increase their overall lifetime benefit from Social Security. Delaying might not be optimal, however, if there are reasons to think your life expectancy might be shortened. In that case, delaying can reduce your overall lifetime benefit.

Reading Check

Your friend Gladys has been coming to you for advice about Social Security, since you have retired recently. Gladys asks you what would happen if she and her husband were to start receiving Social Security early. Uncomfortable with giving her that advice on your own, who would you recommend Gladys speak to? If you were to tell Gladys what would happen if she starts her Social Security benefits early, what would you tell her? How could Gladys maximize her benefits?

Special Filing Strategy: Restricted Application

In addition to the decision on *when* to file, Michael and Jenny need to consider *how* they file for Social Security benefits. If you were born before January 1, 1954, you could have additional filing options like Michael and Jenny. At their Full Retirement Ages, Jenny could elect her own benefit, while Michael could file but restrict his application to only his spousal benefit (50% of Jenny's PIA, or $600.)

Filing a restricted application temporarily lowers Michael and Jenny's annual benefit: $21,600 instead of $43,200. Because Michael is not electing his own benefit, his own benefit will increase annually at 8% per year, up to $3,168 per month at age 70. The total annual income at age 70 would be at least $54,416—more than 20% higher than if Michael and Jenny elected their own benefits at age 66.

The Bipartisan Budget Proposal Act of 2015 limited the use of restricted applications, and all but eliminated the "file and suspend" strategy. You may not qualify for these strategies.

1.11 Paying for Long-Term Care Expenses with Social Security

One of the most important reasons to maximize your Social Security benefit is to provide the maximum amount of monthly income should you require long-term health care. Most people who receive long-term care receive Social Security benefits. These benefits can provide a consistent stream of income that can be put toward care. However, given the current cost and inflation figures for long-term care, your check will not cover all of your costs.

When Social Security retirement benefits are not enough to pay for long-term care, the gap will have to be filled with other sources of income. Some people choose to purchase insurance policies designed to pay privately for care. Private pay options include indemnity policies, short-term and long-term care insurance policies, or accelerated payments from life insurance or annuity policies.

If you find yourself in a position with no other resources to pay for care, programs like Medicaid are able to provide additional funding. Medicaid is administered by each state, and many states require you to assign your Social Security retirement benefit to the state or a third-party health-care company to qualify. This is in addition to stringent financial requirements to "spend down" your assets. (The Veterans Aid and Attendance program does not have the spend-down requirement as of this writing. For more on that program, see chapter 4 in *The Complete Cardinal Guide*.)

Medicaid planning is extremely complex, with state-specific rules. Consider seeing an attorney who specializes in asset protection and Medicaid qualification. Consulting an attorney and a Certified Financial Planner™ professional together will help provide an additional level of security to an asset protection plan with a contingency for long-term care funding.

Reading Check

Why is it important to maximize Social Security retirement benefits? What are some of the private pay options that are available to people preparing for long-term care? How do Medicaid and Social Security interact with each other in regards to long-term care?

———•———

Cornelius and Arthur are having a conversation while fishing early one morning. Cornelius tells Arthur that his kids have been worrying him about long-term care. Arthur tells Cornelius not to worry about it, since Social Security would pay for it. Is Arthur right? Explain.

Preparation for Social Security Planning

OBTAIN A SOCIAL SECURITY EARNINGS REPORT FOR YOUR SPOUSE (IF APPLICABLE) AND YOURSELF.

On page 2, full retirement age is

Self: ....

Spouse: ....

Projected retirement date: ..../......../20.................

Spouse: ..../......../20.................

Do you or your spouse plan to work .... part time or .... full time in retirement?

KEY QUESTIONS

- What is Medicare? What are its Parts?

- When do most people become eligible for Medicare?

- What options are available for going on Medicare?

- How does Medicare cover prescriptions?

- What are Medicare Supplement Policies?

- Why would I change my Medicare Supplement policy?

- What is "LIS," or Extra Help?

- What is an Income-Related Monthly Adjustment Amount (IRMAA)?

- How does Medicare pay for Long-Term Care?

Corresponds to Chapter 3, "Medicare: Excellent Health Insurance, But It's Not Long-Term Care," in The Complete Cardinal Guide.

2.1 What is Medicare?

Medicare is the federal health insurance program for people who are 65 or older, people with disabilities, and people with end-stage renal disease. It is broken down into four Parts: A, B, C, and D.

When Lyndon B. Johnson became president after the death of John F. Kennedy, he was determined to address many serious domestic problems. One of the most important was an increasing number of elderly Americans dealing with very limited health-care coverage or none at all. In addition, at that time older people had little to no protection against the rising costs of health care. A year and a half into his presidency, Johnson worked with Congress to enact Medicare in 1965.

Prior to the creation of Medicare, only half of Americans over the age of 65 had any kind of hospital insurance. Very few had group insurance covering the cost of physicians or surgery. People with pre-existing conditions would be classified as high risk, and many of these disabled and elderly individuals were having their policies terminated by private insurance companies. Furthermore, they could be excluded from purchasing coverage in the future, or forced to buy in to high-risk insurance policies with high premiums.

There were government programs that provided financial aid for health care before Medicare, but they were very limited and difficult to access. These programs had very strict eligibility requirements and narrow coverage. Today, more than 55 million elderly or disabled Americans are covered under Medicare.

In 2003, President George W. Bush signed into law the Medicare Prescription Drug, Improvement, and Modernization Act. This law, also called the Medicare Modernization Act, completely overhauled Medicare for the first time in its 38-year history. It created the Part D Prescription Drug Insurance Program, bringing together funds from the consumer, the insurance companies, and the government to help cover the increasing cost of prescription medications. The law also created the Medicare Advantage program, called Part C.

2.2 Medicare Eligibility and Enrollment Periods

Most people become eligible for Medicare the first day of the month of their 65th birthday. If you have retired and earned Medicare eligibility through your own work history or your spouse's, you should enroll in Medicare. Part A covers hospitalization and outpatient medical services like chemotherapy, and has no ongoing premium. Part B, which pays for services provided by doctors and for routine procedures or operations, is important to have, especially if you do not have creditable coverage from another insurance provider. Together Parts A and B make up Original Medicare.

For most people, Part B has a monthly premium near the national average of $134. Higher-income Medicare beneficiaries will pay a surcharge on Parts B and D (see below). These surcharges, called Income-Related Monthly Adjustment Amounts (IRMAAs), are applied to individuals and couples with above-average incomes.

If you're already receiving Social Security benefits or Railroad Retirement Board benefits, you will automatically be enrolled into Parts A and B unless you opt out. People under 65 and disabled will become eligible for Parts A and B after they receive disability benefits from Social Security or certain disability benefits from the Railroad

Retirement Board for 24 months. Those with more extreme medical conditions like Amyotrophic Lateral Sclerosis (ALS), also known as Lou Gehrig's disease, will become eligible for Parts A and B as soon as their disability benefits begin. If you are eligible but not receiving these benefits, you will need to enroll by contacting the Social Security Administration. Many people apply for Social Security and Medicare benefits at the same time, but that is not required. If you do, your Medicare Part B premium will be deducted from your Social Security check. If you delay Social Security benefits but elect Medicare, you will have to pay for your Part B premium via a bank draft or a quarterly check.

Initial Enrollment Period

You can sign up for Part A and/or Part B during a seven-month period beginning three months before you turn 65. This is called the **Initial Enrollment Period.** If you turn 65 on the first of the month, your Medicare benefits start the first day of the prior month. If you enroll in Part A and/or Part B during the month you turn 65 or during the last three months of your Initial Enrollment Period, your Medicare coverage will be delayed and you may be without coverage. If you are still working at 65 and are covered by group insurance (which can provide creditable insurance coverage), delaying Part B can save you money and preserve your **Open Enrollment** rights for Medicare Supplemental coverage (see below).

If you wait to enroll outside of your Initial Enrollment Period you can be penalized and your coverage can be delayed for months. In addition to paying higher premiums for a lifetime, you risk being without coverage for months. The **General Enrollment Period** for Medicare runs from January 1 to March 31; coverage starts in July. There are also some exceptions, known as **Special Enrollment Periods**. If you miss your chance to sign up in the initial enrollment period, this is when you can sign up.

Special Enrollment Period

If you or your spouse is still working, you will have a chance to sign up for Medicare outside of your Initial Enrollment Period by qualifying for a Special Enrollment Period. If you or your spouse didn't sign up for Medicare when you were first eligible because you both were covered under a group health plan based on current employment, you could enroll into Medicare under a Special Enrollment Period. It is important to act quickly once you decide to retire or otherwise lose coverage from a current employer. Special Enrollment Periods are one way to avoid late enrollment penalties or gaps in coverage.

Fig. 2.1

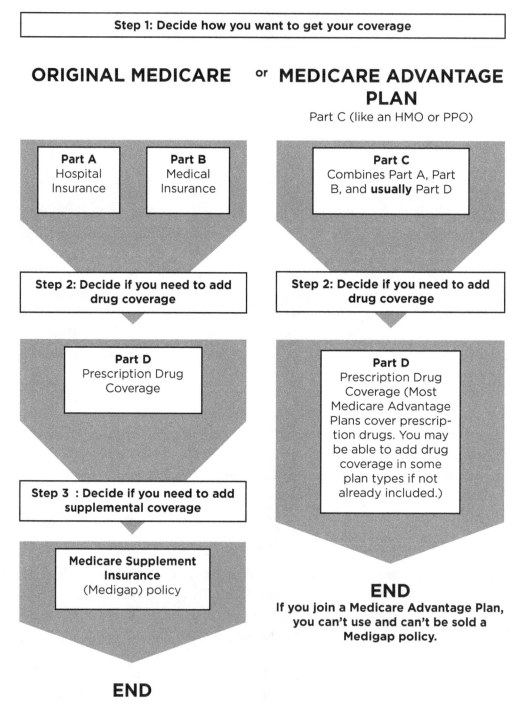

START

Step 1: Decide how you want to get your coverage

ORIGINAL MEDICARE or **MEDICARE ADVANTAGE PLAN**
Part C (like an HMO or PPO)

Part A
Hospital
Insurance

Part B
Medical
Insurance

Part C
Combines Part A, Part B, and **usually** Part D

Step 2: Decide if you need to add drug coverage

Step 2: Decide if you need to add drug coverage

Part D
Prescription Drug Coverage

Part D
Prescription Drug Coverage (Most Medicare Advantage Plans cover prescription drugs. You may be able to add drug coverage in some plan types if not already included.)

Step 3 : Decide if you need to add supplemental coverage

Medicare Supplement Insurance
(Medigap) policy

END
If you join a Medicare Advantage Plan, you can't use and can't be sold a Medigap policy.

END

2.3 Original Medicare versus Medicare Advantage

Once you are eligible for Medicare you will need to decide how you receive your benefits. Most people choose **Original Medicare** with Parts A and B. Another option is to choose Part C, which provides an alternative to Original Medicare called **Medicare Advantage** (see chart on facing page). Medicare Advantage plans have low premiums and various out-of-pocket co-payments and co-insurance costs. These plans are similar to an HMO plan that requires the use of a particular network of doctors. Part D prescription drug coverage can be bought separately if you use Original Medicare (and some Medicare Advantage plans), or these benefits may be included in a Medicare Advantage plan.

Under Original Medicare your benefits and network are provided and administered by the Centers for Medicare and Medicaid Services (CMS). An Advantage plan provides similar Part A and Part B benefits but is administered by a private insurance company. Medicare Advantage plans often operate very differently from Original Medicare. Their main advantage is they cost less than Medicare Supplement insurance.

As with Medicare Parts A and B, delaying enrollment into Part D can create a lifetime penalty. Part D also has an Initial Enrollment Period and an Annual Enrollment Period (from October 15 to December 7) each year. Medicare Advantage and Part D prescription drug plans are offered and administered by many different insurance companies and can be changed annually by the insurance carrier. The prices of certain procedures or medications can change from year to year inside the same plan. Therefore, it is important to annually review your Medicare Advantage (Part C) and Part D plans with a qualified insurance agent or your senior citizens' health insurance society in your state.

Reading Check

Charles has been talking to his 69-year-old friend Paul about his upcoming 65th birthday, which is two months away. Charles asked Paul when he should start looking at signing up for Medicare. What should Paul tell Charles? What would be different if Charles is still working and has group insurance?

Charles wants to know if there are options outside of Original Medicare. What should Paul tell Charles?

———•———

After your monthly book club meeting, your friend Georgetta confides in you that she is confused about how Medicare works and all of the different Parts. How are the Parts different from each other?

2.4 How to Choose a Medicare Supplement Plan (Medigap)

In November 1990, President George H. W. Bush and Congress took action to standardize Medicare supplement policies. Most states have accepted this modernization.

If you decide you want to participate in Original Medicare instead of Medicare Advantage, you have several important decisions to make. One of the most important is whether or not you need a "Medigap" policy. Formally known as a **Medicare Supplement plan, a Medigap policy functions as secondary insurance to pay health-care costs that Medicare Parts A and B approve but don't cover.** One of the first pieces of information you will receive regarding Medicare Supplement polices is a government guidebook, *Choosing a Medigap Policy: A Guide to Health Insurance for People with Medicare.* This booklet is published annually by the Centers for Medicare and Medicaid Services (CMS). It is jointly developed by CMS and the National Association of Insurance Commissioners.

One of the most important sections in *Choosing a Medigap Policy* compares the 10 Medicare Supplement/Medigap policies that are available in 47 states. (Minnesota, Wisconsin, and Massachusetts have not accepted the standardized set of Medicare Supplement policies.) These 10 different policies are lettered Plan A through Plan N. **Since these plans have been standardized by the federal government, each lettered policy is the same from company to company.** The only difference between them is the cost of the plan.

Medicare beneficiaries who apply for Medigap during their Initial Enrollment Period are eligible for an **Open Enrollment**, which allows them to apply for *any* Medigap plan offered by any insurance carrier, without having to answer any health underwriting questions. Pre-existing conditions cannot preclude you from receiving benefits or qualifying for coverage. This Open Enrollment period is similar to guaranteed-issue rights. If you delayed your Part B benefits due to having creditable coverage from an employer, your Open Enrollment period is also delayed until you begin Part B. It is very important to use your Open Enrollment right correctly.

Sixty percent of Americans who own a Medicare Supplement policy have Plan F, the most complete Medigap plan. Plan F provides coverage for each "gap" in Medicare coverage (the Part A and B deductibles, co-payments, co-insurance, and even certain excess charges). Plan G offers the next-best coverage and provides the best value for most people. Plan G does not include the Part B deductible.

Fig 2.2

Benefits	Medicare Supplement Insurance (Medigap) Plans									
	A	B	C	D	F	G	K	L	M	N
Medicare Part A and hospital costs (up to an additional 365 days after Medicare benefits are used)	100%	100%	100%	100%	100%	100%	100%	100%	100%	100%
Medicare Part B coinsurance or copayment	100%	100%	100%	100%	100%	100%	50%	75%	100%	100%
Blood (first 3 pints)	100%	100%	100%	100%	100%	100%	50%	75%	100%	100%
Part A hospice care coinsurance or copayment	100%	100%	100%	100%	100%	100%	50%	75%	100%	100%
Skilled nursing facility care coinsurance			100%	100%	100%	100%	50%	75%	100%	100%
Part A deductible		100%	100%	100%	100%	100%	50%	75%	50%	100%
Part B deductible			100%		100%					
Part B excess charges					100%	100%				
Foreign travel emergency (up to plan limits)			80%	80%	80%	80%			80%	80%

In the following example, Ruth is a single 70-year-old woman who doesn't smoke. Ruth learned from a Medicare Supplement Premium Comparison Report that other insurance carriers were offering her same plan for a lower price. It's easy to compare premiums with very little personal information: age, zip code, tobacco use, and gender are all that's required.

Ruth's report included prices for Plans F and G. Plan G is considerably less expensive, mainly because it lacks coverage for the annual Part B deductible. Still, even if Ruth paid the deductible her total cost would be less than for Plan F.

Fig. 2.3

Plan F Rates for Ruth[*]

Company	Monthly Rate	Company	Monthly Rate
Old Surety	$119.79	Thrivent Financial	$173.25
American National Life	$126.17	American Republic	$175.15
CSI Life	$127.75	Senitnel Security	$175.59
Greek Catholic Union of the USA	$131.63	UnitedHealthcare	$177.77
Companion Life	$133.21	American Rebublic Corp	$178.94
Medico Corp Life	$136.63	Gerber Life	$179.09
Aetna	$136.95	Globe Life and Accident	$189.00
Combined	$139.40	Reserve National	$203.05
New Era	$140.62	Equitable Life & Casualty	$205.09
Americo Financial Life & Annuity	$141.92	Bankers Fidelity	$207.74
IAC	$142.31	Amercian Republic Corp	$210.52
American National Life	$143.37	BCBS of North Carolina	$215.50
HumanaDental	$143.48	Gerber Life	215.77
Manhattan Life	$144.00	Humana	$216.94
GPM Life	$144.51	United Healthcare	$223.67
Central States Indemnity	$144.58	Humana	$226.02
Loyal Christian Benefit Association	$145.11	Reserve National	$233.50
Sentinel Security	$147.86	Colonial Penn	$233.64
USAA	$148.41	Standard Life and Accident	$238.28
UnitedHealthcare	$148.45	United American	$242.00
American Retirement	$148.88	Bankers Fidelity	$251.24
Equitable Life & Casualty	$154.00	United Commercial Travelers	$256.13
American Retirement	$154.08	American Retirement	$258.59
Mutual of Omaha	$159.99	Colonial Penn	$259.49
Americo Financial Life and Annuity	$163.21	Physicians Mutual	$265.12
Oxford	$163.85	UnitedHealthcare	$267.66
State Farm	$168.64	Colonial Penn	$288.22

For zipcode 25711, accessed April 1, 2017
Provided by CSG Actuarial, csgactuarial.com

Fig. 2.4

Plan G Rates for Ruth[*]

Company	Monthly Rate	Company	Monthly Rate
CSI Life	$98.33	American Retirement	$130.21
American National	$99.79	Americo Financial	$136.76
Loyal Christian Benefit Association	$101.56	Bankers Fidelity	$138.30
IAC	$106.48	Equitable Life & Casualty	$150.25
Greek Catholic Union	$108.52	Gerber Life	$150.98
Aetna	$109.21	Reserve National	$151.95
Sentinel Security	$109.86	Thrivent Financial	$152.46
Central States Indemnity	$110.25	Colonial Penn	$171.26
Medico Corp	$110.54	Reserve National	$174.75
GPM Life	$111.92	Standard Life & Accident	$175.93
Mutual of Omaha	$112.71	Gerber Life	$181.92
Equitable Life &Casualty	$112.75	Colonial Penn	$190.18
American National	$113.40	United Commercial Travelers	$192.25
New Era	$114.80	BCBS of North Carolina	$205.25
Bankers Fidelity	$115.25	Colonial Penn	$211.20
Manhattan Life	$116.25	Physicians Mutual	$214.38
Americo Financial	$118.92	United American	$231.00
HumanaDental	$120.70	American Retirement	$233.69

*For zipcode 25711, accessed April 1, 2017
Provided by CSG Actuarial, csgactuarial.com

Notice the varying costs in both premium comparison reports. Every Medicare Supplement policy offered in each plan provides the same benefits, but at very different costs. You are able to switch Medigap plans anytime during the year, subject to qualifying based on your health history. If you are healthy enough, you could switch plans annually to save on costs without sacrificing your coverage.

Premiums can be compared through some state insurance department websites, and many independent insurance agents can produce a report that covers multiple companies' policies. We suggest that you find a trustworthy agent who can help you understand your options and find the lowest-cost plan.

Reading Check

While having coffee with your sister Ivy, she tells you she was able to change her Medicare Supplement to a less expensive plan. How was Ivy able to change her supplement? Will she get the same kind of coverage?

2.5 How Does Medicare Prescription Drug Coverage (Part D) Work?

Medicare offers prescription drug coverage to all beneficiaries. Even if you don't take many prescriptions, you should consider joining a Medicare drug plan. That's because if you decide not to join one when you are first eligible, you will likely pay a late enrollment penalty if you delay without demonstrating you have creditable coverage. This penalty will last as long as you have prescription drug coverage. People who have other kinds of creditable coverage or receive assistance from the Extra Help program (see below) can avoid late enrollment penalties.

To get Part D coverage, you must enroll in a plan approved by Medicare. Plans can vary in cost and the specific drugs covered. There are two ways to obtain Medicare Part D: Prescription Drug Plans (PDP) and Medicare Advantage Plans (MAPD).

Medicare Prescription Drug Plans add drug coverage to Original Medicare. You must have Part A or Part B to enroll in a Medicare Prescription Drug Plan.

Medicare Advantage Plans combine benefits from Part A, Part B, and Part D into one plan. You must have Part A and Part B to join a Medicare Advantage Plan, and not all Medicare Advantage Plans offer prescription drug coverage.

If you choose a Medicare Advantage plan you will receive your Medicare benefits from a private insurance company. You will still need to pay for Part B and any additional Medicare Advantage premium. Unlike Medicare Supplement policies, the premium for Medicare Advantage policies can be deducted from your Social Security check.

Reading Check

Larry and Connie have been trying to determine their Medicare Prescription Drug Plan coverage. Larry tells Connie he found a PDP that would provide her with drug coverage. Connie told Larry that she doesn't want to have multiple policies; she already has a Medigap policy. How can Connie get drug coverage without buying a PDP?

2.6 The Extra Help Program or Low-Income Subsidy (LIS)

Extra Help is a Medicare program that helps people with limited resources pay Medicare prescription drug costs. If you qualify for this low-income subsidy program, the government will pay your Part B premium and reduce your Part D drug co-payments. (Note: This program is different from Medicaid.) In 2015, the qualifying threshold for a single person was annual income less than $17,665 and financial resources less than $13,640. Financial resources include money in a checking or savings account, stocks, bonds, mutual funds, and Individual Retirement Accounts. Your home, car, household items, burial plot, and up to $1,500 in prepaid burial expenses or life insurance policies do not count toward your financial resources. For a married couple who lived together and had no other dependents, those income limits were $23,895 and $27,250, respectively, in 2015. These figures can change from year to year.

In some situations you can qualify for Extra Help even if your income is above the limits established by Medicare. If you still work, live in Alaska or Hawaii, or have dependents living with you, you might be eligible for Extra Help. If you qualify for Extra Help and join a Medicare Prescription Drug Plan, you will get help paying for your monthly premium, yearly deductible, co-insurance, and co-payments. You will have no "donut hole" or coverage gap, and late enrollment penalties can be waived. Those on Extra Help have the option to switch Medicare Advantage plans and Prescription Drug Plans at any time during the year, even outside of the Annual Enrollment Period. Any change they make will take effect the first day of the following month.

Reading Check

Charlotte has been struggling to pay her Part D premium. She does a bit of research and learns about Extra Help. What are the income and asset limits that Charlotte would have to meet to qualify for Extra Help? What would they be if she was married?

2.7 Higher-Income Beneficiaries

People who have a higher income than the average Medicare beneficiary will notice higher premiums for their Part B and Part D coverage. These income-related monthly adjustment amounts (IRMAAs) are based on your most recently filed tax return (for calendar year 2017, information from your 2015 tax return on file with the IRS is requested by Medicare). These surcharges affect less than 5% of Medicare recipients, so most people don't pay a higher premium. Details of these adjustments are covered in Module 7: Income Taxes.

Reading Check

Orson and Amelia tell you they have heard about different Medicare rules for those who have a higher income. What would you tell them?

2.8 Medicare and Long-Term Care

It is an easy mistake to think that government programs like Social Security and Medicare will fully protect retirees from poverty and health-care costs. Assuming that all health-care costs are covered is a major financial mistake. **Medicare does not pay for long-term care,** the non-skilled medical care that people require when they are unable to perform the necessary activities of daily living. Long-term care can be extremely expensive and is not covered by Medicare, Medicare Advantage, or Medicare Supplements. Government benefits like Tricare and the Federal Employees Health Benefits (FEHB) also do not cover long-term care costs.

Reading Check

Beatrice runs into you at the supermarket. You haven't seen each other in ages. While catching up, she mentions that her brother-in-law Ted is going to need some kind of long-term care. Beatrice says she is thankful that Ted has Medicare because they don't know if they could afford that care without it. Is Beatrice correct in this thinking? Why or why not?

PLANNING FOR MEDICARE

Under 65

Month/Year I turn 65: ..../20..........

Spouse ..../20.............

Current Health Insurance: ....

65+

Part A Start Date: ..../.........../..........

Part B Start Date: ..../.........../..........

Part D Plan: ....

Medicare Supplement:

Spouse

Part A Start Date: ..../.........../..........

Part B Start Date: ..../.........../..........

Part D Plan: ....

Medicare Supplement:

KEY QUESTIONS

- What is Long-Term Care (LTC)?

- What kinds of Long-Term Care insurance are available to consumers?

- How do I plan for Long-Term Care?

- Will Medicaid pay for Long-Term Care?

- Who can help me plan for Long-Term Care?

Corresponds to Chapter 4, "Long-Term Care: There's an Appropriate Strategy for Every Family,"
*in **The Complete Cardinal Guide.***

3.1 The Importance of Long-Term Care (LTC)

You can't predict all the risks you will face throughout your lifetime, let alone when they will occur. For some situations that involve unknown risks, insurance policies can transfer the risk away from you and to an insurance company. For example, you buy homeowner's insurance to protect yourself in case of a natural disaster, and you purchase auto insurance to help mitigate the risk you assume when you drive a car. You can prepare for your death or the passing of a loved one by purchasing life insurance and burial plots. Long-term care insurance can provide additional financial protection for the unknowns inherent in retirement planning.

Today there are better options for long-term care insurance than there were only 10 years ago. Halfway through his second term, President George W. Bush prevailed on Congress to take action to deal with a crisis around retirement financing. Pensions were facing financial stress, and in addition sick and ailing Americans were paying high taxes on large withdrawals from investments to pay for long-term care. The Pension Protection Act of 2006 (PPA) helped fix these problems by ensuring that distributions from annuity and life insurance policies used to pay for long-term care insurance and expenses would be treated as tax-free, as long as the policies and distributions are considered "qualified." This law created a large market for new hybrid or "linked-benefit" policies that combine tax-free LTC benefits with the underlying guarantees of an annuity or life insurance policy. These new policies, along with traditional long-term care insurance, provide additional strategies for smarter long-term planning.

These qualified traditional long-term care insurance policies, and the hybrid policies, have similar triggers that must be met before the policy pays any benefits. The inability to perform two of the six activities of daily living (ADL) without substantial assistance or supervision will trigger benefits. **These common daily activities are: bathing, dressing, eating, toileting, transferring, and continence**. The type of health care that provides assistance for these activities is called "personal care."

The main focus of long-term care planning is to provide adequate funding to pay for an extended period of personal care and to preserve the accustomed standard of living for the healthy spouse. Long-term care planning provides a road map for how to pay for care as your health deteriorates. Previously, extended care for the activities of daily living was provided in a nursing home. Today, care can be provided in group centers and in assisted living and nursing home environments. These businesses provide certified nursing assistants and other non-skilled health-care workers who can supervise or assist a patient in need. However, more and more people are able to receive care at home with the assistance of licensed home health-care agencies. Nowadays, conditions like Parkinson's disease, a prolonged illness, and/or a cognitive disorder like Alzheimer's disease can be addressed in a more comfortable atmosphere at home.

Prior to beginning long-term care planning with clients, we want to prepare them mentally for the task at hand. Developing an objective understanding is key to making a rational long-term care plan. The Certification in Long-Term Care (CLTC®) training designation has advisors ask potential clients to consider the following:

- A rational person will understand there is a likelihood that he or she could live a long life.

- A rational person will understand that if he or she lives a long life, the chances of becoming frail or forgetful are real.

- A rational person will understand that paying for long-term care will undoubtedly impact his or her finances and family.

Once you can come to terms with these realities, you can face long-term care planning more objectively.

Reading Check

Doris is thinking about purchasing a long-term care insurance policy. The one she is looking at mentions Activities of Daily Living. Curious, she asks the agent helping her, Sean, what those are. What should Sean tell Doris about the Activities of Daily Living?

3.2 Types of Long-Term Care

This section defines long-term care and describes the various settings in which Americans receive it. Long-term care is also known as "elder care" or "nursing home care," despite the fact that many people who receive it are under 65, and many folks receive it in a setting other than a nursing home.

Long-Term Care
Includes a wide range of medical and support services for people with a degenerative condition (for example, Parkinson's disease, or those that occur after a stroke), a prolonged illness (cancer), and/or a cognitive disorder (Alzheimer's). Long-term care is not necessarily medical care, but rather custodial care.

Home Health Care
Services in the client's home. Can include nursing care, social services, medical care, homemaker services, and occupational, physical, respiratory, or speech therapy.

Assisted Living Facility
A residential living arrangement that provides personal care and health services for people who need some help with activities of daily living but don't need the level of help given by a nursing home.

Nursing Home
Provides skilled, intermediate, and custodial nursing care for residents who need a higher level of medical care than that provided by an assisted living facility.

Adult Day Care
Care given during the day at a community-based center for adults who need help or supervision with daily activities.

Respite Care
Care provided by a third party to relieve family caregivers.

Reading Check

Mary has been diagnosed with dementia. She has been trying to hide the effects of her failing memory from her family because she doesn't want to be placed in a nursing home. Is a nursing home her only option to receive care?

3.3 Long-Term Care Planning

Throughout this section, we review pricing and benefit examples of two short-term care policies, one traditional long-term care policy, six versions of hybrid long-term care, and a brief financial plan for self-insurance. Information is given for a 55-year-old female and a 70-year-old female who are funding $3,000 of monthly benefits with a 5% compounded inflation factor. This level of benefits partially insures the risk of long-term care. Prices for males are generally less for long-term care. Couples applying together can generally receive large discounts, because the insurance companies know that when two spouses live together, one will generally care for the other for a while.

The policies presented below are similar in that they all pay monthly benefits for the long term and they all have a premium that is paid either up front or over time. They differ in the health criteria you have to meet to qualify and the design of the policy.

The underwriting boxes below the policy descriptions show the actual health questions the insurance company asks you. Full underwriting means they ask you a thorough set of questions, and a yes answer is cause for deeper investigation to determine if you are insurable. Simplified underwriting asks a limited set of questions, where a yes answer means you are not insurable and if all the answers are no, you get the policy.

3.3.1 Short-Term Care

"**SHORT-TERM CARE INSURANCE** gives your family almost a year of $3,000 monthly payments while they figure out how to make self-insurance work for you. It may not sound like much, but I can tell you that the families who are collecting on it are very grateful for the time it buys them. Short-term care insurance pays for home health care as well as facility care. The health criteria are much easier to meet than for traditional long-term policies, which makes short-term care available to more people" (chapter 4, *The Complete Cardinal Guide*).

Policy 1

This is a short-term care policy paying benefits up to 360 days or 52 weeks. The health qualifications (underwriting) are simplified, the premiums affordable, and it provides coverage for the first year of care.

Daily Benefit: $100 • Monthly Benefit: $3,000 • Maximum Benefit: $36,000
Benefit Period: 360 Days • Waiting Period: 0 Days • Inflation: None
Death Benefit: $0 • Unisex Rates • No Couples Discount
To Add Male Spouse: Double the Price

In addition to the $100 daily benefit for nursing home or assisted living care, this coverage pays $1,200 weekly, up to $62,400 annually, for home health care on an indemnity basis if minimum services are received. Receiving benefits on an indemnity basis means that you receive the benefit as a flat rate as soon as you qualify for it, unlike reimbursement, where the company simply pays you back for what you spent.

Fig. 3.1

Age 55 Female		Age 70 Female	
Monthly Premium	Annual Premium	Monthly Premium	Annual Premium
$53.71	$644.52	$136.24	$1,634.88

This coverage will pay a daily benefit for confinement in a nursing or assisted living facility, provided you cannot perform two or more Activities of Daily Living (ADLs) or have a cognitive impairment. No prior hospital stay is required.

The home health rider pays a benefit for each week you receive three or more professional home care service visits of at least one hour per visit, provided you cannot perform two or more ADLs or have cognitive impairment.

Policy 1 Underwriting (Simplified)

The following are examples of questions asked by the insurance company during the underwriting process:

Fig. 3.2

---

1. **Are you currently:**
   - confined to a hospital or nursing facility?
   - bedridden or receiving any type of home health care?
   - dependent on a walker, cane, wheelchair, or motorized mobility device?
   - requiring assistance in performing everyday activities such as walking, eating, dressing, shopping, housekeeping, toileting or bathing?

2. **Do you have diabetes:**
   - that requires the use of 50 or more units of insulin?
   - with any complications resulting from the diabetes (including neuropathy, heart or artery blockage, retinopathy)?
   - Do you have insulin dependent diabetes in conjunction with a heart disorder (other than high blood pressure)?

3. **Within the past 12 months, have you:**
   - been advised by a medical professional to have treatment, further evaluation, diagnostic testing or have test results pending?
   - been diagnosed or treated by a medical professional for any type of seizure?

4. **Within the last 12 months have you been advised by a medical professional that surgery may be required within the next year for any existing health condition including joint replacement?**

5. **Within the past 12 months have you been recommended or advised by a medical professional to have treatment or counseling for alcohol or drug abuse?**

6. **Within the past 24 months have you:**
   - been prescribed the use of oxygen by a medical professional?
   - had any type of amputation caused by disease?
   - been treated for transient ischemic attack (TIA), Cerebrovascular Accident (CVA) or stroke?
   - been hospitalized three or more times for any reason?
   - had any lung or respiratory disorder requiring the use of a nebulizer or oxygen, or three or more medications for lung or respiratory disorder?
   - been diagnosed or treated by a medical professional for a mental or nervous disorder excluding anxiety or mild depression?

7. **Within the past 36 months have you been diagnosed or treated by a medical professional or had surgery for any of the following:**
   - congestive heart failure, kidney disease, cirrhosis, Paget's disease, lupus, or any connective tissue disorder?
   - internal cancer (including breast cancer and prostate cancer), leukemia, lymphoma, or melanoma?
   - Alzheimer's disease, dementia, Parkinson's disease, cerebral palsy, multiple sclerosis, or any other neurological or neuromuscular disorder?
   - Acquired Immune Deficiency Syndrome (AIDS), AIDS related complex (ARC), or tested positive for the Human Immunodeficiency Virus (HIV)?

Policy 2

This is a short-term care policy paying benefits up to 350 days. The health qualifications (underwriting) are simplified, the premiums affordable, and it provides coverage for the first year of care. This coverage provides a couples discount. When husband and wife are issued policies together, each receives a 10% discount.

Daily Benefit: $100* • Maximum Benefit: $35,000
Benefit Period: 350 Days
Waiting Period: 0 Days • Inflation: None • Death Benefit: $0
Unisex Rates • 10% Couples Discount • To Add Male Spouse: +80%

Policy covers nursing home, assisted living, adult day care, and home health care. This is a reimbursement policy and any unused portion of the $100 daily is forfeited.

Fig.3.3

Age 55 Female		Age 70 Female	
Monthly	Annually	Monthly	Annually
$37.50	$450	$115.42	$1,385

Fig 3.4

1. **Do you require supervision or assistance with Activities of Daily Living such as walking, eating, bathing, dressing, toileting, moving into or out of a bed or chair, or with taking medication?**

2. **Have you ever had an organ transplant (other than corneal) or a defibrillator implanted?**

3. **Do you ever use a hospital bed, walker, wheelchair, quad cane, motorized personal transport, chair lift, or oxygen?**

4. **Have you ever been diagnosed with a terminal illness which is expected to end your life within the next 12 months?**

5. **In the past 12 months:**
    - Have you been confined in a hospital, or have you had heart surgery including bypass, angioplasty, stent placement, or heart valve surgery?
    - Have you had a balance disorder or have you fallen more than 2 times?

6. **In the past two years:**
    - Has a medical professional scheduled or advised you to have surgery requiring general anesthesia, or undergo testing and you have not done so?
    - Have you resided or been advised to reside in a Nursing Home or Assisted Living Facility?
    - Have you received or been medically advised to receive Home Health Care or Adult Day Care services?
    - Have you received Worker's Compensation, Social Security Disability benefits, or other long-term disability benefits?

7. **In the past two years, have you had, been diagnosed with, received treatment, or taken medication for any of the following conditions?**
    - Alzheimer's disease, dementia, or memory loss
    - Acquired Immune Deficiency Syndrome (AIDS) or Human Immunodeficiency Virus (HIV)
    - Amyotrophic Lateral Sclerosis (ALS), Multiple Sclerosis, Muscular Dystrophy, Parkinson's disease, paralysis, or myasthenia gravis
    - Psychosis or Schizophrenia
    - Diabetes with complications such as retinopathy (eye disease) or neuropathy (numbness/tingling in hands or feet)
    - Internal cancer, leukemia, lymphoma, or melanoma
    - Osteoporosis with related fracture(s)
    - Systemic lupus, kidney failure, cirrhosis of the liver, hydrocephalus, or connective tissue disease
    - Stroke or cerebrovascular accident (CVA), transient ischemic attack (TIA), congestive heart failure, atrial fibrillation, peripheral vascular disease, or cardiomyopathy
    - Amputation due to disease, alcohol or drug abuse

Short-Term Care Policy Comparison

Both short-term care policies have similar benefits for confinement, but they offer very different benefits for home health care. With Policy 1, the home health-care benefits and maximum are separate from your use of facility care. With Policy 2, you can use the $100 daily and the $35,000 maximum for either facility care or home health care, but not both. The health criteria to qualify for Policy 2 are easier to meet than for Policy 1, and it has generous height and weight thresholds. On the other hand, Policy 1 has no height and weight requirements.

Note that short-term care policies are not available in all states.

3.3.2 Traditional Long-Term Care

"**TRADITIONAL LONG-TERM CARE INSURANCE** is just what it sounds like: Thinking ahead, you purchase a policy that pays $3,000 monthly once you need long-term care and lasts for several years up to the policy maximum. Caveat: Such a policy must be purchased well in advance of the foreseeable need. Most companies now offer a maximum of ten years of benefits; we typically sell our clients two to five years, which keeps the premium more affordable. The policy pays benefits for either home health care or facility care and allows you to bank the unused portion, which makes the benefits last longer. I also recommend inflation protection.

"There are some disadvantages to a traditional long-term care plan. If you pay in to the policy for several years and never use it, all your money has gone to pay other policyholders who needed benefits. The company can raise the premium—with the approval of insurance regulators—perhaps when you are vulnerable and can't afford it. Also, health qualifications for traditional long-term care insurance have become tougher over the years. Underwriting will request records from your doctor and possibly any specialists you have seen, will run a report of your prescriptions, and will do a little memory test that will seem silly over the phone. Some companies even send a nurse to your house to examine you" (chapter 4, *The Complete Cardinal Guide*).

Policy 1

Following is an example of a traditional long-term care policy. This policy provides $3,000 monthly for either home health care or facility care, and pays that amount until you reach the policy maximum of $150,000. These benefits increase 3% annually for inflation. This policy qualifies for the partnership program in most states (see section 3.4 below). Women pay more than men for this policy. The cost to add a male spouse the same age qualifying for a couple's discount is just 13% more in premium. This policy has extensive health questions (full underwriting) and qualifying for it may be difficult.

Single • Partnership Qualified • Monthly Benefit: $3,000*
Maximum Benefit: $150,000 • Benefit Period: 50 Months
Waiting Period: 90 Days • Inflation: 3% Compound • Death Benefit: $0
Gender Distinct Rates • To Add Male Spouse: +13% /+12%

Monthly amount covers nursing home, assisted living, and home health care.

Fig 3.5

	Age 55 Female		Age 70 Female	
	Monthly	Annually	Monthly	Annually
Total Premium	$223.00	$2,473.00*	$394.00	$4,377.00*

Paying the premium annually in advance saves you on the premiums.

Policy 1 Underwriting (Full)

The following are examples of questions the insurance company might ask during the underwriting process:

Fig 3.6

---

1. **What is your height?**

2. **What is your weight?**

3. **Have you ever used tobacco?**

4. **Have you ever received medical treatment, counseling, or been hospitalized for drug use?**

5. **Do you regularly consume 4 or more alcoholic beverages per day, or do you drink 5 or more drinks per day, 1 or more days per week?**

6. **Have you ever received medical treatment, counseling, or been hospitalized for alcohol use?**

7. **Do you have, for your use, a handicap parking sticker or handicap license plate?**

8. **Have you been diagnosed or treated by a member of the medical profession as having Acquired Immune Deficiency Syndrome (AIDS), AIDS Related Complex (ARC), or Human Immunodeficiency Virus (HIV) Infection (symptomatic or asymptomatic)?**

9. **Do you currently qualify for payment or are you receiving payment benefits under Medicaid (not Medicare), disability income plan, workers' compensation, Social Security disability, or any federal or state disability plan?**

10. **To the best of your knowledge has your biological mother, father, or sibling been diagnosed with Alzheimer's disease or another form of dementia?**

11. **Have you ever been diagnosed with, treated for, tested positive for, or been given medical advice by a member of the medical profession for sleep apnea?**

12. **Do you currently have any of the following?**

    - Electric scooter
    - Hospital bed
      Nebulizer
    - Oxygen (including supplemental CPAP use)
    - Quad cane

    - Respirator
    - Stairlift
    - Walker
    - Wheelchair

13. **Do you require assistance or supervision of another person or a device of any kind for any of the following?**

    - Bathing
    - Toileting
    - Dressing
    - Eating

    - Medication management
    - Getting in and out of a chair or bed
    - Inability to control your bowel or bladder

---

14. **Have you ever had, been diagnosed as having, or received medical advice or medical care from a physician or health care provider for any of the following?**

- Alzheimer's Disease
- Amyotrophic Lateral Sclerosis (ALS, Lou Gehrig's Disease)
- Cancer (except basal or squamous cell skin cancers, or stage I/A bladder, thyroid, breast, or prostate cancers) in the past 2 years
- Chronic Hepatitis
- Chronic Obstructive Pulmonary Disease (COPD), Emphysema, or Chronic Bronchitis and have used tobacco in the past year
- Cirrhosis
- Connective Tissue Disease
- Dementia
- Diabetes and currently taking more than 50 units of insulin daily, or with peripheral neuropathy, numbness, tingling or decreased sensation in your feet, retinopathy or history of stroke, ministroke or a TIA
- Huntington's Chorea
- Hydrocephalus
- Kidney failure or received dialysis
- Memory Loss
- Mental Retardation
- Mild Cognitive Impairment
- Ministroke or Transient Ischemic Attack (TIA) in the past year, single episode stroke in the past 2 years, 2 or more strokes or TIAs, or you have not fully recovered or continue to have weakness, decreased sensation or loss of function from a stroke or TIA
- Multiple Myeloma
- Multiple Sclerosis (MS)
- Muscular Dystrophy
- Myasthenia Gravis
- Organ Transplant
- Organic Brain Syndrome
- Paralysis
- Parkinson's Disease
- Psychosis
- Schizophrenia
- Scleroderma
- Systematic Lupus

15. **Are you scheduled for a visit with a medical professional within the next 6 months?**

16. **Have you received physical, occupational, or speech therapy in the past 6 months?**

17. **Have you used insulin in the past 6 months?**

18. **Within the past 6 months have you been confined to, used, or been advised to have any of the following?**

- Residential care, assisted living, or adult day care facility services
- Nursing home or home health care services

19. **Have you been seen by your physician, health care provider, or any specialist more than three times in the past 12 months?**

20. **Have you received inpatient or outpatient treatment at a hospital, surgical center, or rehabilitation facility in the past 12 months?**

21. **Have you had an unplanned weight change in the past 12 months?**

22. **Are you age 65 or older and has it been more than 2 years since you have had a doctor's visit which included a head to toe physical examination with blood work (basic metabolic chemistry panel)?**

23. **Have you been hospitalized or had surgery in the last 3 years?**

24. **In the past 3 years has a medical professional referred you to a specialist for additional consultation, testing, or surgery?**

25. **Have you been advised by a member of the medical profession in the last 5 years to have surgery which has not yet been completed?**

26. **During the last 10 years, have you ever used unlawful drugs, or used prescription medications other than as prescribed by your doctor?**

27. **Have you ever received any advice, treatment, consultation, or diagnosis from a physician or health care provider for any of the following conditions?**

- Anemia, Blood Clotting or Blood Disease/Disorder
- Arthritis, Broken Bone, Back, Spinal Stenosis, Scoliosis, Bone or Joint Disorder
- Balance Disorder, Difficulty Walking, or Falls
- Cancer, Leukemia, or Lymphoma
- Chronic Pain, Amputation, or Polymyalgia Rheumatica
- Depression, Anxiety, or other Mental Disorder
- Diabetes
- Dizziness/ Vertigo or Fainting
- Fibromyalgia, Weakness, or Fatigue
- Head Injury, Nerve Damage, or other Neurological Disease/Disorder
- Heart Rhythm, Heart Valve, Coronary Artery, Heart Disease/Disorder
- Hepatitis or Liver Disease/Disorder
- High Blood Pressure
- Immune System Disease/Disorder
- Incontinence or other Bowel or Bladder Disease/Disorder
- Kidney Disease/Disorder
- Lung Disease/Disorder
- Osteoporosis or Osteopenia
- Seizure, Epilepsy, or Tremors
- Shingles
- Stroke, Transient Ischemic Attack, Aneurysm, Carotid, or Circulatory Disease/Disorder
- Vision Disorder

28. **In the past 5 years have you been diagnosed with, treated for, had testing for, or consulted with a medical professional for conditions or symptoms not listed above?**

3.3.3 Hybrid Long-Term Care

"**HYBRID LONG-TERM CARE** is the fastest-growing segment of the long-term care business. Sharing some features of life insurance, hybrid long-term care insurance is more consumer friendly and addresses several of the big problems of traditional long-term care insurance. First, if you don't use it during your lifetime, there is a death benefit that enables your beneficiaries to receive the unused portion when you die. Many of these policies also have a return-of-premium feature that allows you to get your premiums back (without interest) if you ever want to cancel your insurance. Second, the company can never raise the premium. Third, the money can be used for a variety of care settings, including in-home and rehabilitation care. The trade-off is that you pay for a hybrid policy all up front. The cost is generally $100,000 or more, and one of the companies lets you use IRA money to fund it. You do have to meet health qualifications, but they are more lenient since you are paying up front" (chapter 4, *The Complete Cardinal Guide*).

The Pension Protection Act of 2006 made it possible for life insurance and annuity companies to add long-term care benefits to regular life and annuity policies. It also provides that charges for long-term care inside the policy are not taxed. The law was intended to expand the availability of tax-favored long-term care benefits through the use of cash values and death benefits in insurance policies.

Policy 1

This policy provides similar benefits to the traditional long-term care policy shown above. Since it is a single-premium life insurance policy, you pay the large premium up front, and if you do not use all of the benefit during your lifetime, your heirs will receive a benefit after you pass away. It only costs 9% more to additionally cover a male spouse the same age on a survivorship policy. The first $75,000 of benefits does not have 3% inflation. The second $75,000 of benefits has the 3% inflation rider. This policy has full underwriting with extensive health questions.

> Monthly Benefit: $3,000 • Maximum Benefit: $150,000
> Benefit Period: 50 Months • Waiting Period: 60 Days
> Inflation: 3% Compound (Rider Only)

Fig 3.7

Age 55 Female	Age 70 Female
Death Benefit: $75,000 Less Any Long-Term Care Benefits Paid • To Add Male Spouse: +9%	Death Benefit: $75,000 Less Any Long-Term Care Benefits Paid • To Add Male Spouse: +13%
SINGLE PREMIUM FOR BASE LIFE INSURANCE POLICY	SINGLE PREMIUM FOR BASE LIFE INSURANCE POLICY
$32,641	$49,811
SINGLE PREMIUM FOR EXTENSION RIDER	SINGLE PREMIUM FOR EXTENSION RIDER
$12,103	$16,342
TOTAL	TOTAL
$44,744	$66,153

Policy 2

This policy is similar to the one listed above, but it allows you to pay for most of it using IRA funds. Rolling over IRA funds is less desirable for benefit payouts but is very attractive to clients who have IRA funds they are not using for retirement income. This policy has full underwriting with extensive health questions.

> Monthly Benefit: $3,000 • Maximum Benefit: $150,000
> Benefit Period: 50 Months • Waiting Period: 60 Days
> Inflation: 3% Compound (Rider Only)

Fig 3.8

Age 55	Age 70
Death Benefit: $75,000 • To Add Male Spouse: +9%	Death Benefit: $75,000 • To Add Male Spouse: +13.5%
IRA ROLLOVER INTO AN ANNUITY	IRA ROLLOVER INTO AN ANNUITY
$34,922	$50,772
NON-QUALIFIED SINGLE PREMIUM	NON-QUALIFIED SINGLE PREMIUM
$12,103	$16,342
TOTAL	TOTAL
$47,025	$67,114

Policy 3

This policy is straight single-premium life insurance, with a substantial single premium and no additional premium for riders. The long-term care benefit maximum starts at $180,000 and grows over time as the cash value in the policy grows. That is how inflation is accounted for. This policy pays an indemnity benefit, which means you don't need to send in receipts of expenses to collect benefits. If you pass away not having used all your benefits for long-term care, your heirs will receive the unused portion as a life insurance benefit. The health standards (underwriting) are easier to meet than for traditional long-term care, but more difficult than for short-term care. If at any point you want your original money back, you can have it.

Straight Single-Premium Life with LTC

Monthly Benefit: $3,000 (Home Health)/$5,000 (Facility Care)
Maximum Benefit: $180,000 • Benefit Period: 60 Months/36 Months
Waiting Period: 0 Days • Inflation: Policy Performance

- 1/60th of death benefit paid each month during chronic illness: $3,000/month

- 1/36th of death benefit paid each month during confinement: $5,000/month

- Indemnity benefit, not reimbursement

- Optional full refund of premium for life of policy

Fig 3.9

Age	Age 55		Age 70	
	Single Premium: $76,271 Initial Death Benefit: $180,000		Single Premium: $111,111 Initial Death Benefit: $180,000	
	GUARANTEED LTC BENEFIT	PROJECTED BENEFIT	GUARANTEED LTC BENEFIT	PROJECTED BENEFIT
80	$180,000	$260,163	$180,000	$204,451
90	$180,000	$287,398	$180,000	$226,058
100	$180,000	$326,549	$180,000	$255,938

Policy 3 Underwriting

In between simplified and full underwriting. A simple phone interview issues this policy. Less difficult to qualify for than full underwriting.

Fig 3.10

Fig 3.11

<table>
<tr><td colspan="2">1. Have you ever had</td></tr>
<tr><td>
<ul>
<li>AIDS/HIV</li>
<li>ALS (Lou Gehrig's Disease)</li>
<li>Alzheimer's</li>
<li>Cerebral Palsy</li>
<li>Coronary Artery Disease in combination with Diabetes</li>
<li>Cystic Fibrosis</li>
</ul>
</td>
<td>
<ul>
<li>Dementia</li>
<li>Down's Syndrome</li>
<li>Ebola</li>
<li>Huntington's Disease</li>
<li>Mental Incapacity/ Organic Brain Syndrome</li>
<li>Muscular Dystrophy</li>
<li>Organ Transplant (other than Kidney donor)</li>
</ul>
</td></tr>
</table>

1. Have you ever had

- AIDS/HIV
- ALS (Lou Gehrig's Disease)
- Alzheimer's
- Cerebral Palsy
- Coronary Artery Disease in combination with Diabetes
- Cystic Fibrosis
- Dementia
- Down's Syndrome
- Ebola
- Huntington's Disease
- Mental Incapacity/ Organic Brain Syndrome
- Muscular Dystrophy
- Organ Transplant (other than Kidney donor)

2. Last Year or Less

- Unable to perform Activities of Daily Living for 7+ consecutive days during the past 6 months; dressing, eating, ambulating, toileting, or bathing
- Current hospitalization or confined to a bed/ nursing facility
- Hospice care received or recommended
- Unexplained loss over 20 pounds

3. Last 5 years

- Alcohol/Drug abuse
- Aneurysm
- Anorexia/Bulimia
- Cancer or recurrence and or metastasis of Cancer
- DWI/DUI
- Heart Attack
- Malignant Melanoma
- Multiple Sclerosis
- Narcolepsy
- Pacemaker
- Post-traumatic Stress Disorder
- Psychosis
- Schizophrenia/Bipolar Disorder
- Stroke/TIA
- Suicide Attempt
- Tuberculosis

4. Last 10 years

- Cardiomyopathy
- Chronic Obstructive Pulmonary Disease
- Cirrhosis of the Liver
- Congestive Heart Failure
- Coronary Artery Disease
- Diabetes with insulin use
- Emphysema/Chronic Bronchitis
- Heart Valve Replacement
- Hemochromatosis
- Hepatitis other then Type A
- Hydrocephalus (water on the brain)
- Immune System Disorder
- Kidney failure or dialysis
- Leukemia/Lymphoma
- Oxygen use (or recommended use)
- Paralysis (hemiplegia, paraplegia, quadriplegia)

Height	Weight Min	Weight Max
5'0"	85	217
5'1"	88	224
5'2"	91	232
5'3"	94	239
5'4"	97	247
5'5"	100	255
5'6"	103	263
5'7"	106	271
5'8"	109	279
5'9"	112	287
5'10"	115	296
5'11"	119	304
6'0"	122	313
6'1"	126	322
6'2"	129	331
6'3"	133	340
6'4"	136	349
6'5"	140	358
6'6"	143	367

Policy 4

This policy has very easy underwriting because it uses your money in the beginning to pay you back benefits. After your money is used up paying for long-term care, then the benefits come out of the insurance company's money. It pays out either two or three times your initial payment, depending on your health (underwriting) when you applied. The premiums below include 5% inflation.

> **Single Premium Deferred Annuity with 2x LTC or 3x LTC**
> **Benefit Period: 72 Months • Inflation: 5% Compound**
> **Waiting Period: 60 Days for Confinement/0 Days for Home Health Care**

The "monthly" benefit in the tables below is the long-term care benefit you will receive each month at that age. The "LTC Max" benefit is the most long-term care benefit you will receive in your lifetime. These benefits grow over your lifetime because of the 5% compounded inflation factor.

Fig 3.12 (Part A & B)

Age 55				
	2X		3X	
	Single Premium: $125,000 Death Benefit: $107,250		Single Premium: $92,500 Death Benefit: $74,099	
AGE	MONTHLY INCOME	LTC MAX	MONTHLY INCOME	LTC MAX
55	$3,000	$216,045	$3,046	$220,317
70	$5,894	$321,588	$6,032	$301,162
80	$9,601	$455,405	$9,825	$546,285
90	$15,683	$373,142	$16,003	$843,111
100	$25,473	$1,027,574	$26,067	$1,326,446

Fig 3.12 (Part C & D)

Age 70				
	2X		3X	
	Single Premium: $130,000 Death Benefit: $109,708		Single Premium: $95,000 Death Benefit: $72,264	
AGE	MONTHLY INCOME	LTC MAX	MONTHLY INCOME	LTC MAX
70	$3,029	$218,725	$3,000	$216,233
80	$4,698	$278,830	$4,653	$295,607
85	$5,996	$325,555	$5,939	$357,313
90	$7,653	$385,190	$7,579	$436,067
100	$12,465	$558,439	$12,346	$664,860

Fig 3.13

Qualification for 2x

1. **Are you currently hospitalized, confined to a bed, or residing in an Assisted Living Facility?**

2. **In the last 12 months have you applied for any long-term care policy or long-term rider that was declined or postponed?**

3. **Are you currently using, or in the past 12 months, have you been medically advised by a Healthcare Professional to use, any of the following?**
   - Care in a nursing facility
   - Dialysis machine
   - Home Health care services
   - Hospice Care
   - Hospital bed
   - Motorized scooter
   - Multi-prong cane
   - Oxygen
   - Stair Lift
   - Walker
   - Wheelchair

4. **Do you require assistance or supervision in performing any of the following activities?**
   - Bathing
   - Dressing
   - Eating
   - Getting in or out of a chair or bed
   - Managing your bowel or bladder
   - Taking medication
   - Toileting
   - Walking

5. **In the last 7 years**
   - Alzheimer's disease or dementia
   - Autoimmune disorder/disease such as Lupus, Systemic Scleroderma, CREST syndrome Connective Tissue disease
   - Cirrhosis
   - Hepatitis
   - Huntington's disease
   - Lou Gehrig's disease (ALS)
   - Mental incapacity or retardation
   - Mild cognitive impairment (MCI)
   - Multiple Sclerosis
   - Muscular dystrophy
   - Organ transplant other than cornea or kidney
   - Organic brain syndrome
   - Paralysis
   - Parkinson's disease
   - Recurrent memory loss
   - Smoking in conjunction with Emphysema, COPD
   - Spinal Stenosis or Chronic Back pain with use of narcotic medication
   - Stroke or Multiple Transient Ischemic Attack (TIA)

Fig 3.14

Qualification for 3x

6. In the last 12 months

- Aneurysm
- Any fall resulting in a fracture
- Cardiomyopathy
- Congestive heart failure
- Heart bypass surgery
- Heart valve replacement
- Hospitalized overnight 2 or more times
- Multiple falls
- Seizure or convulsion
- Tremors
- Vascular surgery

7. In the last 5 years

- Alcohol or drug abuse or dependency
- Blood clotting deficiency
- Cancer other than non-melanoma skin cancer
- Hodgkin's disease or other lymphoma
- Leukemia
- Von Willebrand disease
- Hospitalization for depression, bipolar disorder or any other psychiatric disorder
- Idiopathic thrombocytopenic purpura (ITP) or essential thrombocythemia
- Smoking with peripheral vascular disease, diabetes, or renal disease

8. In the last 7 years

- Bipolar disorder, schizophrenia, or other psychosis
- Chronic kidney failure
- Diabetes currently treated with insulin
- Diabetes with a history of TIA, Stroke, Neuropathy, kidney disease, peripheral vascular disease, or congestive heart failure
- Kidney or cornea transplant
- Myasthenia gravis
- Rheumatoid arthritis requiring use of narcotic medication
- Rheumatoid arthritis with joint deformity
- Rheumatoid arthritis with joint replacement
- TIA with history of heart disease

Policy 5

This is a traditional Universal life policy that offers a choice of paying annual premiums for life, 10 years of premiums, or a single premium. It has no inflation, so you may want to buy a larger policy in the first place. This policy requires full underwriting, which means qualifying for it might be difficult.

Universal Life Insurance with Long-Term Care Rider
Monthly Benefit: $3,000 • Maximum Benefit: $150,000
Benefit Period: 50 Months • Waiting Period: 90 Days
Death Benefit: $150,000 • Inflation: None

Fig 3.15

Age 55	Age 70
ANNUAL PAY FOR LIFE	ANNUAL PAY FOR LIFE
$2,432	$5,490
ANNUAL PAY FOR 10 YEARS	ANNUAL PAY FOR 10 YEARS
$5,209	$9,419
SINGLE PAY-ONE TIME	SINGLE PAY-ONE TIME
$49,717	$92,668

Policy 6

This policy works best for clients who have major health conditions that would disqualify them for the other policies that require underwriting. A large premium is paid into an annuity to purchase a deferred or future monthly income. The longer you wait to start the income, the larger the income you receive. The income is guaranteed to last for your entire lifetime. If and when you qualify for long-term care, the monthly income is doubled, and stays doubled as long as you need long-term care or for five years, whichever is shorter. The maximum benefit is equal to the cash value in the policy, meaning when you run out of money, you run out of benefits.

Single-Premium Deferred Annuity with Guaranteed Withdrawal
Rider Enhanced for Long-Term Care
Maximum Benefit: Cash Value
Benefit Period: Cash Value • Waiting Period: 0 Days
Inflation: None • Death Benefit: Equals Cash Accumulation
Minus Income Withdrawals
Use Qualified (IRA) or Non-qualified Funds to Pay the Premium

---

Fig 3.16

Age 55			Age 70		
Single Premium: $100,000					
AGE	MONTHLY INCOME	MONTHLY LTC INCOME	AGE	MONTHLY INCOME	MONTHLY LTC INCOME
65	$720	$1,440	80	$956	$1,991
75	$1,498	$2,995	90	$1,632	$3,263

The only health question asked is, "Do you currently need human assistance with bathing, dressing, transferring, toileting, eating, or continence?"

3.3.4 Self-Insurance

"**SELF-INSURANCE** means providing the entire long-term care bill yourself from your income and assets. This requires careful planning so your family members will know what to do when and if you start to need outside care. It is much better to have a financial planner doing this work for you now than to have a nursing home administrator doing these calculations when you are being admitted.

"We start with your Social Security check and any other income you receive that is reliable. We deduct ongoing monthly expenses that won't go away if you are receiving care. The net number is applied toward the long-term care bill and what's left is the monthly dollar amount needed to fill the gap. Then we add up your financial assets and begin paying the gap number out of interest first, principal second. We recommend using your remaining IRA money first, because the assisted living or nursing home bill will give you a big tax deduction as a medical expense. This hit me while doing my Mom's taxes after she was confined. She had $66,000 in medical expense deductions and very little income to deduct it against. We sell annuity products from several different insurance companies that allow you to defer income taxes on current earnings until you draw the money out. (An annuity is a series of payments you receive over a period of time, open specified as for life.) Some of the companies enhance the monthly income available to you if you use it to pay for long-term care. **Self-insurance may be your only option if your health conditions limit your options for buying insurance**" (chapter 4, *The Complete Cardinal Guide*).

A long-term care self-insurance solution for people who are over age 74 and already receiving care is now available. It is offered by a large A+-rated insurance company. George is 79 years old and had a major stroke. He is currently receiving care in an assisted living facility. His stepdaughter, who legally serves as his power of attorney, recently applied for this policy on George's behalf. George had $292,000 in a savings account earning very little interest. The insurance company did what is called reverse underwriting and determined that for that amount of money, they can write a policy to pay him $3,020 monthly for the rest of his life. This income will pay 60% of his assisted living rent. If George dies in the first two years, the premium will be partially refunded to his heirs. If he lives for 15 years, the insurance company will pay out a lot more than was paid in (chapter 4, *The Complete Cardinal Guide*).

Hybrid Policy Comparison

All of these hybrid policies were formed after the Pension Protection Act was passed in 2006. They start out with a lump sum of money and make payments to a beneficiary if there is unused money in the account. Some of these policies require additional payments after the initial lump sum, some do not. The health questions also differ between policies, making some easier to qualify for than others. The differences among all hybrid policies stem from the fact that they are developed by insurance companies that are using their creativity to solve this problem in their own unique way.

Reading Check

Sue is 70 years old and does not feel she can pay a monthly premium for long-term care. She does have $100,000 in a CD at the bank paying less than 1% interest. What type of long-term care policy would you recommend for Sue?

3.4 Medicaid and Long-Term Care

Medicaid—the federal government health insurance program for low-income people—will provide long-term care (in a Medicaid-approved bed) after you have spent your assets down to a very low level (it varies by state). You are not allowed to give your assets away to qualify for Medicaid.

Most states have a partnership program that allows you to purchase a partnership-approved long-term care insurance policy. A partnership policy allows your estate to retain a higher level of assets and still go on Medicaid. Listed below is a chart listing which states participate.

Fig 3.17

STATE	EFFECTIVE DATE	POLICY RECIPROCITY
Alabama	3/1/2009	Yes
Alaska	Not Filed	--
Arizona	7/1/2008	Yes
Arkansas	7/1/2008	Yes
California	Original Partnership	--
Colorado	11/1/2008	Yes
Connecticut	Original Partnership	Yes
Delaware	11/1/2011	Yes
District of Colombia	Not Filed	--
Florida	1/1/2007	Yes
Georgia	1/1/2007	Yes
Hawaii	Pending	--
Idaho	11/1/2006	Yes
Illinois	Pending	--
Indiana	Original Partnership	Yes
Iowa	1/1/2010	Yes
Kansas	4/1/2007	Yes
Kentucky	6/16/2008	Yes
Louisiana	10/1/2009	Yes
Maine	7/1/2009	Yes
Maryland	1/1/2009	Yes
Massachusetts	Proposed	--
Michigan	Work Stopped	--
Minnesota	7/1/2006	Yes
Mississippi	Not Filed	--
Missouri	8/1/2008	Yes

STATE	EFFECTIVE DATE	POLICY RECIPROCITY
Montana	1/1/2009	Yes
Nebraska	7/1/2006	Yes
Nevada	1/1/2007	Yes
New Hampshire	2/16/2010	Yes
New Jersey	7/1/2008	Yes
New Mexico	Not Filed	--
New York	Original Partnership	Yes
North Carolina	3/7/2011	Yes
North Dakota	1/1/2007	Yes
Ohio	9/10/2007	Yes
Oklahoma	7/1/2008	Yes
Oregon	1/1/2008	Yes
Pennsylvania	9/15/2007	Yes
Rhode Island	7/1/2008	Yes
South Carolina	1/1/2009	Yes
South Dakota	7/1/2007	Yes
Tennessee	10/1/2008	Yes
Texas	3/1/2008	Yes
Utah	Not Filed	--
Vermont	Not Filed	--
Virginia	9/1/2007	Yes
Washington	1/1/2012	Yes
West Virginia	7/1/2010	Yes
Wisconsin	1/1/2009	Yes
Wyoming	6/29/2009	Yes

Last updated March 2014

Reading Check

Alvin has been researching long-term care that might be suitable for him. He believes that Medicaid might be a viable option for him. What might have led Alvin to think that? If he doesn't meet the income requirements for Medicaid, are there other options out there for Alvin? During his research Alvin also learned about Partnership Programs. How do Partnership Programs work?

3.5 Veterans Aid and Attendance

Veterans and their spouses requiring long-term care could qualify for the Veterans Aid and Attendance program. This special program pays an additional monthly pension benefit to qualifying beneficiaries who need home health care or are housebound. Like Medicaid, a number of qualifications must be met to participate in the program.

Veterans who served during wartime and received an other-than-dishonorable discharge could qualify for the program. Additional financial and asset qualifications must also be met. Though most senior centers around the country offer assistance completing the application, that assistance is severely limited. The volunteers are prevented from giving financial or legal advice. The planning services provided by professionals may carry a charge, but the Department of Veterans Affairs prohibits charging a fee to help file the Aid and Attendance paperwork. You can search for accredited representatives and attorneys on the VA website: https://www.va.gov/ogc/apps/accreditation/.

Reading Check

Who should seek help for Veterans Aid and Attendance? Can someone be charged for receiving help filling out an application for Veterans Aid and Attendance? What are some of the criteria established by Veterans Affairs for Veterans Aid and Attendance?

PLANNING FOR LONG-TERM CARE

If my spouse or I need care, we prefer that care take place:

.... at home or .... in assisted living

If one or more of my adult children or nieces/nephews need to look after my affairs when I am incapacitated, that person is/are:

Power of Attorney ....

Health-Care Power of Attorney..

HIPAA Release ....

From the examples shown in this module; I am most interested in

.... Short-Term Care

.... Traditional Long-Term Care

.... Hybrid Long-Term Care

.... Self-Insurance

| **IRA**
(INDIVIDUAL RETIREMENT ACCOUNTS)

KEY QUESTIONS

- What is an IRA?

- How do IRAs work?

- How are a Roth IRA and a traditional IRA different? How are they alike?

- When am I required to start Required Minimum Distributions (RMD)?

- What is the process for making investments into a traditional IRA or Roth IRA?

- How do IRAs figure into my long-term care planning?

Corresponds to Chapter 5, "Assets: Your IRA, 401(k), and Pension Plan,"
in The Complete Cardinal Guide.

4.1 The Origin of IRAs

Traditional Individual Retirement Accounts, or IRAs, allow you to save for retirement on a tax-advantaged basis. Traditional IRAs use "pre-tax" funds that can grow while you defer paying taxes on them. Ordinary income taxes are due only when withdrawals are made from a traditional IRA. The IRA was created in 1974 with the passage of the Employee Retirement Income Security Act (ERISA) championed by President Gerald Ford. ERISA was put in place to protect non-government employees by creating standardized vesting schedules for private pension plans like a 401(k) and other employer-sponsored benefits. It also provides individuals and small business owners with access to retirement savings plans like the

Simplified Employee Pension (SEP-IRA) and the Savings Incentive Match Plan for Employers (SIMPLE IRA and SIMPLE 401[k]).

One impetus for ERISA was the bankruptcy of companies, which left employees without access to pensions. A prominent example was the automobile manufacturer Studebaker, which failed and closed in the 1960s. The Employee Retirement Income Security Act does not require private employers to set up expensive and burdensome pension plans; instead it allows for the creation of defined contribution plans that use tax-deferred arrangements and IRAs to help employees invest for retirement. These accounts enable employees to earmark funds for retirement, and allow capital gains and dividend income to compound on a tax-deferred basis until the funds are withdrawn from the account during retirement.

The Roth IRA was created by the Taxpayer Relief Act of 1997 and named for its chief sponsor, Senator William Roth of Delaware. The Roth IRA's principal difference from a traditional IRA is that rather than allowing a tax deduction when the money is deposited into the IRA, the tax benefit is granted when the money is withdrawn during retirement. You pay no income taxes on money coming out of a Roth IRA. Tax-free retirement income is now a reality. It is now also possible to convert traditional IRA money (taxable) to Roth IRA money (tax-free). The bad news is that you must pay all the income taxes due to make the conversion.

Reading Check

How long have traditional IRAs been around? What is the main difference between a traditional IRA and a Roth IRA?

4.2 America's IRA Expert

Ed Slott became "America's IRA expert" by training financial advisors, CPAs, attorneys, insurance agents, and consumers on the ins and outs of planning for and then using an IRA for its intended purpose: living off it in retirement. IRAs enjoy tax preferences or "loopholes" that allow taxes to be postponed, or now even the possibility of tax-free income with the Roth IRA. The Internal Revenue Service is very unforgiving when a taxpayer neglects or remains ignorant of the regulations about transferring or "rolling over" an IRA, taking money out of an IRA or failing to do so, and leaving your IRA to your heirs.

Consumers are focused on the accumulation of the balance in their IRA or 401(k) while they are still working. At retirement, or just before retirement, the focus changes from accumulation to distribution (or living off of it). Now come the decisions about how you plan to distribute your IRA and make it last the rest of your life. Many financial advisors, attorneys, CPAs, and insurance agents who advise retirees on IRA and 401(k) decisions during retirement are not well trained in the IRS rules for handling them. Mistakes are costly and many times cannot be reversed.

In this module, we discuss transfers and rollovers, beneficiary designations, age 70½ required minimum distributions, and Roth conversions, and we issue a warning about stockpiling money in an IRA to leave to your kids.

Reading Check

Why do retirement planning experts take specific training on IRA distributions?

4.3 Transferring Your IRA

Your IRA/401(k)/pension must remain in your name, and your name alone, as long as you are alive. Your money and securities must be held by a custodian (like a bank or stock brokerage) who makes sure all the IRS rules and reporting requirements are followed exactly. You may choose another custodian or your plan might require you to move the money and securities to another custodian. This is referred to as a rollover or transfer. There is a way for you to take a check for the balance (possibly after income taxes are withheld). You then have 60 days to get it redeposited into a new IRA or face income taxes on the whole amount. New IRS rules are in place limiting the frequency of this "60-day exemption," making it even more complicated.

Our advice is: "Don't take the risk. Have the money transfer directly to the new custodian without it ever coming into your direct possession." Some employers or retirement plans will tell you that they have to make the check out to you when leaving their plan. The check can be made out to XZY IRA CUSTODIAN COMPANY for the benefit of MARY SMITH. This will satisfy your employer and the IRS. If it takes an example to convince you, see Rebecca's story in chapter 5 of *The Complete Cardinal Guide*.

Reading Check

When moving IRA/401(k) money into a new IRA, move the money from _____ to _____.

4.4 IRA Beneficiary Forms

Beneficiary forms must be updated regularly. Your beneficiaries will need to pay income tax on this inheritance (unless the IRA is a Roth). With the right advice and proper account titling, they can stretch the income taxes over their lifetime.

A spouse beneficiary is treated more favorably than a non-spouse beneficiary. A spouse can leave the IRA titled in the original holder's name or retitle the IRA in their own name. A non-spouse beneficiary must retitle the IRA—"Mary Smith, Deceased, IRA FBO Jack Smith"—or cash it out and pay the taxes.

For a good example of the complications involved in effectively using an inherited IRA, see Sybil and Jackson's story in chapter 5 of *The Complete Cardinal Guide*.

Reading Check

Who should you name as the beneficiary of your IRA? Is it OK to forget the use of the beneficiary designation in your IRA and just name them in your will?

4.5 Required Minimum Distributions (RMD)

The US federal tax code gives a significant tax break to people who set aside money in an IRA or other retirement plan. This is to encourage savings for retirement. You can withdraw money as early as age 59½, but you must start withdrawing money by age 70½; this rule is called Required Minimum Distributions, or RMD. Ordinary income tax is due on any money coming out of the IRA unless it is a Roth IRA.

To calculate your RMD, find your IRA balance as of December 31 in the prior year. Calculate your age as of that same date in the current year and find your IRS life expectancy from the table below. Add up all your traditional IRA balances and multiply the total by the percentage that corresponds with your age. You can distribute the money any time during the year and you can withdraw from any IRA you choose. Roth IRAs have no minimum distribution requirements.

Fig 4.1

AGE OF IRA OWNER OR PLAN PARTICIPANT	LIFE EXPECTANCY (IN YEARS)	AGE OF IRA OWNER OR PLAN PARTICIPANT	LIFE EXPECTANCY (IN YEARS)
70	27.4	93	9.6
71	26.5	94	9.1
72	25.6	95	8.6
73	24.7	96	8.1
74	23.8	97	7.6
75	22.9	98	7.1
76	22.0	99	6.7
77	21.2	100	6.3
78	20.3	101	5.9
79	19.5	102	5.5
80	18.7	103	5.2
81	17.9	104	4.9
82	17.1	105	4.5
83	16.3	106	4.2
84	15.5	107	3.9
85	14.8	108	3.7
86	14.1	109	3.4
87	13.4	110	3.1
88	12.7	111	2.9
89	12.0	112	2.6
90	11.4	113	2.4
91	10.8	114	2.1
92	10.2	115+	1.9

AGE OF IRA OWNER OR PLAN PARTICIPANT	RMD AS A % OF ACCOUNT BALANCE	AGE OF IRA OWNER OR PLAN PARTICIPANT	RMD AS A % OF ACCOUNT BALANCE
70	3.65%	93	10.42%
71	3.78%	94	10.99%
72	3.91%	95	11.63%
73	4.05%	96	12.35%
74	4.21%	97	13.16%
75	4.37%	98	14.09%
76	4.55%	99	14.93%
77	4.72%	100	15.88%
78	4.93%	101	16.95%
79	5.13%	102	18.19%
80	5.35%	103	19.24%
81	5.59%	104	20.41%
82	5.85%	105	22.23%
83	6.14%	106	23.81%
84	6.46%	107	25.65%
85	6.76%	108	27.03%
86	7.10%	109	29.42%
87	7.47%	110	32.26%
88	7.88%	111	34.49%
89	8.34%	112	38.47
90	8.78%	113	41.67
91	9.26%	114	47.62
92	9.81%	115+	52.64

A different table can be used if your spouse is more than 10 years younger than you.

Reading Check

After what age must you begin withdrawing money from your traditional IRA?

4.6 Life Insurance and RMD

You can use all or part of the net taxable distributions from an IRA to pay the annual premiums for a life insurance policy. The death benefit on the life insurance policy can equal the balance of the IRA. Life insurance proceeds at your death will be paid to your heirs income tax-free.

Fig. 4.2

IRA Annuity Distributed over 10 Years
Age 70 • Female • $100,000

Taxable IRA Distributions for 10 Years	$11,903
Life Insurance Policy Paid Up for Life	$141,967

$141,967 or more paid to beneficiaries tax-free at death

Another way to leave tax-free money to your heirs is with a Roth IRA. In contrast to a traditional IRA, contributions to a Roth IRA are not tax-deductible. Instead, withdrawals are tax-free and there are no required minimum distributions during your lifetime.

A Roth conversion strategy involves paying the income taxes due on the traditional IRA and then changing it into a Roth. It makes the most sense if you can pay the taxes from other funds and place the entire traditional IRA into a new Roth IRA.

Reading Check

What is the reason IRA funds are not as favorable to heirs as other savings and investments?

4.7 Long-Term Care and IRAs

If you must pay the bill for home health care, assisted living, or nursing home care yourself, we suggest drawing down your IRA balance first before going into other funds. Long-term care expenses are deductible as a medical expense, so you can offset a good bit of the tax liability from the IRA distributions. If you die before spending all your IRA money on long-term care, your heirs will receive money on which the taxes have already been paid.

IRA PLANNER

List all IRA, 401(k), 403(b), 457, and any other accounts:

ACCOUNT	BENEFICIARY(S)

Spouse:

ACCOUNT	BENEFICIARY(S)

I am eligible for a pension from: ....

Spouse is eligible for a pension from: ....

My plan for Required Minimum Distributions after the age of 70½ is:

....

KEY QUESTIONS

- How important is return?

- What is risk management?

- What is an annuity?

- How does age factor into investment strategies?

- How does the likelihood of long-term care affect investments?

- What is the best way to allocate investments to prepare for long-term care?

Corresponds to Chapter 6, "Investing Your Money and Living on it for the Rest of Your Life,"
in The Complete Cardinal Guide.

5.1 A Bit of Investment History

After experiencing the economic growth of the Roaring '20s, many Americans were blindsided by the Stock Market Crash of 1929. For the next 10 years, the United States dealt with its crippled economy, as President Franklin D. Roosevelt led relief and reform measures that helped lessen the suffering of millions of Americans. The crash and the Great Depression made many consumers uncertain about investing in the economy. Fortunately, Roosevelt helped rebuild consumer confidence by ensuring that financial reform was a part of his New Deal, beginning with the Securities Exchange Act of 1934. Prior to this time, Blue Sky Laws regulating securities were only enforced at the state level. The Securities Exchange Act created the Securities and Exchange Commission (SEC), providing for the first time the means for the federal government to protect the public from financial fraud.

Congress continued to establish protections for consumers with the Investment Company Act of 1940. Mutual funds had been created in 1924, but they were largely unregulated. This new law set federal standards for regulating investment companies, and helped build consumer confidence in this fledgling type of security.

Perhaps more important, Congress in 1940 also passed the Investment Advisers Act. This law defined the roles and responsibilities of investment advisors and required them to register with the federal government. All federally registered investment advisory firms are represented by the Investment Adviser Association (IAA). This not-for-profit trade association was founded in 1937 and played a large role in the enactment of the Investment Advisers Act of 1940. The IAA promotes integrity and competence by providing education and other services to members. It also represents those registered investment firms before Congress and the SEC. The firms that are registered with the IAA have to update their paperwork with both the SEC and state securities authorities every year. As a result of that monitoring and oversight, those firms must act in the best interest of their clients, which includes taking into consideration every client's financial position.

Reading Check

Why is the US Securities and Exchange Commission a necessary part of our financial system?

5.2 Risk

Modern portfolio theory rests on the foundation of the relationship between risk and return. Risks are inherent in investing; theory states that efficient investors who take more risk should be compensated with higher potential returns. There are five basic categories of investment risk:

- Market Risk

- Interest Rate Risk

- Inflation (also known as Purchasing Power Risk)

- Liquidity and Marketability Risk

- Credit Risk

As we dig a bit deeper into these basic risks, you should start to understand how various kinds of investments have different risks.

Market Risk

Market Risk is an umbrella term that encompasses different types of risk, which can be categorized into unsystematic and systematic risks. Unsystematic risks are risks that are specific to a company or industry and can be minimized through diversification. Systematic risk is the unavoidable risk that comes with choosing to invest in the market: International politics, war, and economic recession are hazards that cannot be controlled by the investor, but they can definitely increase market risk. The term "volatility" refers to a type of systematic risk, specifically the way that securities prices change on a day-to-day basis. However, while systematic risks cannot be addressed through diversification, they can be mitigated by taking defensive positions, called hedges, to offset an overall bullish position (or vice versa).

Interest Rate Risk

The bond markets are especially sensitive to changes in interest rates. Stocks can also be affected by changes in the interest rate environment, because those rates can influence dividends and growth potential. The world's capital markets are intertwined with interest rates, because interest rates dictate savings account earnings, the cost of loans, and almost every aspect of the economy for the Mom & Pops and Big Business alike. This type of risk cannot be diversified away. It is systematic risk.

Inflation, or Purchasing Power Risk

The prices of goods and services tend to increase over time. The rate of this increase is called inflation. A great example of inflation is the cost of a first-class stamp. The United States Postal Service lowered the price of a first-class stamp in 1919 from 3 cents to 2 cents; today (as of this writing) a stamp costs 49 cents. This increase equates to approximately 3.308% (compounded annually). Economists and financial professionals often use 2.5% or 3% as an estimate of inflation over long periods of time. But this rate can under-represent the inflation of certain goods or services, like health care, and it is not a great predictor of short-term inflation. As the basic cost of living increases over time, it can outpace income growth for working individuals. Retirees are especially prone to purchasing power risk. Health care tends to be one of the largest expenses for retirees, and the cost of health care tends to increase at a greater rate than other goods, like food and gasoline. Cost-of-living adjustments are not guaranteed annually for Social Security. Many pensions lack any type of cost-of-living or inflation adjustments.

Liquidity Risk

One of the most important characteristics of your investments is liquidity. Liquidity refers to how quickly an asset can be converted to cash. Having money when you need it is more valuable than wealth that is tied up, or illiquid. Real estate is the most common example of an illiquid investment, compared to cash, which is completely liquid. Short-term financial needs cannot be met with illiquid investments; keeping an appropriate amount of liquid assets will help protect you from liquidity risk. Marketability is different.

Credit Risk

The risk of default is usually called credit risk. This is the risk that the payor cannot pay the payee. This situation can occur between a lender and a borrower, or between any other two parties when one party cannot live up to their obligations. (Counterparty risk is a form of credit risk.) Buying government securities like Treasury notes and bonds is one way you can avoid credit risk. Investors the world over purchase debt from the United States Treasury because of the "full faith and credit" clause of the Constitution that empowers the government to tax. This clause is seen as a backstop, or guarantee, that gives these Treasury notes and other government debt a "risk-free" status.

Fig 5.1 Risk Comparison

This chart shows the different risks involved with each investment vehicle. Each one varies by what risk they present, but all of them present risk in some way.

INVESTMENT VEHICLE	MARKET RISK	INFLATION RISK	INTEREST RATE RISK	LIQUIDITY RISK	CREDIT RISK
Equities/Stock	High	Low	Moderate	Low	Moderate
Bonds	Low	High	High	Low	Moderate
Equity-Indexed Annuities	Low	Moderate	Low	High	Low
Fixed-Rate Annuities	None	High	Low	High	Low
Bank CDs	None	High	Low	High	None
Cash/Money Market	None	High	None	None	Low
Real Estate	Moderate	Low	Low	High	None
Gold/ Commodities	High	Mixed	Moderate	Low	Low
Options	High	None	Mixed	High	Moderate

Reading Check

Explain the five types of risk. How does each specific type of risk affect the management of your money?

5.3 Equity Investments (Common Stock)

To familiarize you with some of the most common investments, let's look at some of the basic principles behind stocks and bonds.

When news reports or articles refer to the stock price of a given company, they are referring to the common stock issued by the corporation. Though there are other types of stock (e.g., preferred stock), common stock is more popular with ordinary investors.

What Is Stock?

Common stock is a form of ownership in corporations. Stock is sold as a way for a corporation to raise money to finance its operations. By owning shares of the common stock, you are entitled to a share of the company's profits. The first stock company, the Dutch East India Company, was established in 1602 on the Amsterdam Stock Exchange. Today more than 4,000 stocks are traded on major exchanges and another 15,000 are traded directly between investors (over the counter, or OTC).

Are Stocks Risky?

Yes, but not very risky. If a company goes bankrupt and is liquidated, the common stockholders may get paid, but they are last in line after bondholders, preferred stock shareholders, and other debt holders. This is one of the reasons that stocks tend to outperform bonds; common stock has a higher risk of default than bonds do. Common stockholders share the earnings of the company while bondholders receive only the interest stipulated in the bonds.

How Do You Buy Stock?

When a stock corporation is formed, shares are created. These shares can be sold to the public in a variety of ways, including an initial public offering, or IPO. Selling the shares privately or through private placements is another option. Before a stock can be listed on a major exchange like the New York Stock Exchange, certain size and listing requirements must be met.

Reading Check

As a stockholder in a company, what do you own? What do you get in return for your ownership share?

Fig 5.2 Morningstar® Stock Analysis

This is the analysis of one individual stock in the portfolio.

Apple Inc(USD) AAPL

Last Close $	$98.66	
Sales $Mil	$227,535	
Mkt Cap $Mil	$540,403	
Industry	Consumer Electronics USD	
Currency	USD	

Apple Inc designs, manufactures, & markets mobile communication & media devices, personal computers, & portable digital music players, & sells a variety of related software, services, accessories, networking solutions, & third-party digital content.

Morningstar Rating	Fair Value Uncertainty	Fair Value	Economic Moat	Style	Sector
★★★★ As of 07-22-2016	High	$133.00	Narrow	Large Core	Technology

1 Infinite Loop
Cupertino, CA 95014
Phone: +1 408 996-1010
Website: http://www.apple.com

Annual Price High/Low
13.31 28.99 28.51 30.56 46.67 60.96 100.72 82.18 119.75 134.54 112.39
7.18 11.70 11.31 11.17 27.18 44.36 57.86 55.01 70.51 92.00 89.47

Recent Splits 2:1

Price Volatility
147.0 Monthly High/Low
53.0 Rel Strength to S&P 500
19.0 52 week High/Low $ 127.09-89.47
6.0 10 Year High/Low $ 134.54-7.18
2.0

Trading Volume Million 99.0 / 9.0

Growth Rates Compound Annual
Grade: B

	1 Yr	3 Yr	5 Yr	10 Yr
Revenue %	27.9	14.3	29.1	32.6
Operating Income %	35.7	8.8	31.1	45.7
Earnings/Share %	43.0	13.5	33.6	45.1
Dividends %	9.3	73.6	—	—
Book Value/Share %	12.5	6.0	23.5	32.6
Stock Total Return	-19.5	19.7	13.6	28.5
+/- Industry	-1.9	3.3	1.8	11.1
+/- Market	-24.7	8.7	1.1	20.4

Profitability Analysis
Grade: C

	Current	5 Yr Avg	Ind	Mkt
Return on Equity %	39.1	39.0	29.2	21.3
Return on Assets %	17.9	22.7	11.0	6.8
Revenue/Employee $K	2088.5	1960.2	—	861.0
Fixed Asset Turns	10.5	12.4	8.2	7.1
Inventory Turns	58.6	77.4*	14.9	8.9
Gross Margin %	39.8	40.1	34.2	44.5
Operating Margin %	29.4	30.9	21.7	17.5
Net Margin %	22.3	23.4	15.6	13.0
Free Cash Flow/Rev %	24.3	27.5	42.0	15.7
R&D/Rev %	3.5	2.8	2.8	—

Financial Position (USD)
Grade: B

	09-15 $Mil	03-16 $Mil
Cash	21120	21514
Inventories	2349	2281
Receivables	30343	19824
Current Assets	89378	87592
Fixed Assets	22471	23203
Intangibles	9009	9092
Total Assets	290479	305277
Payables	35490	25098
Short-Term Debt	10999	10498
Current Liabilities	80610	68265
Long-Term Debt	53463	69374
Total Liabilities	171124	174820
Total Equity	119355	130457

Valuation Analysis

	Current	5 Yr Avg	Ind	Mkt
Price/Earnings	10.9	14.3	11.5	19.3
Forward P/E	11.2	—	—	21.4
Price/Cash Flow	8.3	10.1	0.2	12.1
Price/Free Cash Flow	10.1	12.0	4.3	41.4
Dividend Yield %	2.2	—	1.8	2.4
Price/Book	4.1	4.8	3.4	2.7
Price/Sales	2.4	3.3	1.8	3.7
PEG Ratio	1.3	—	—	2.8

*3Yr Avg data is displayed in place of 5 Yr Avg

Stock Performance

	2006	2007	2008	2009	2010	2011	2012	2013	2014	2015	YTD
Total Return %	18.0	133.5	-56.9	146.9	53.1	25.6	32.7	7.6	40.0	-2.8	-5.2
+/- Market	2.2	128.0	-19.9	120.4	38.0	23.4	16.7	-24.8	26.3	-4.2	-13.0
+/- Industry	7.1	69.4	-0.6	41.8	11.7	15.8	2.9	-3.3	6.6	1.7	-2.4
Dividend Yield %	—	—	—	—	—	—	1.0	2.1	1.7	1.9	2.2
Market Cap $Mil	72981	174039	75997	190983	297089	377547	499696	500741	643120	583613	540403

Financials (USD)

	2006	2007	2008	2009	2010	2011	2012	2013	2014	2015	TTM
Revenue $Mil	20681	26499	33038	46708	78283	127841	164687	173992	193800	234988	227535
Gross Margin %	29.0	33.2	35.2	40.1	39.4	40.5	43.9	37.6	38.6	40.1	39.8
Oper Income $Mil	3025	5213	6275	13364	21487	43303	55111	49252	59286	71155	66864
Operating Margin %	12.7	17.9	22.2	27.4	28.2	31.2	35.3	28.7	28.7	30.5	29.4
Net Income $Mil	2428	4073	4858	9358	16639	32982	41747	37031	44462	53731	50678
Earnings Per Share $	0.32	0.56	0.77	1.30	2.16	3.95	6.31	5.68	6.45	9.22	9.02
Dividends $	0.00	0.00	0.00	0.00	0.00	0.00	0.38	1.63	1.81	1.98	2.08
Shares Mil	6143	6225	6315	6349	6473	6557	6617	6522	6123	5793	5648
Book Value Per Share $	1.66	2.73	3.68	5.64	8.48	11.74	19.37	19.77	19.15	21.53	23.82
Oper Cash Flow $Mil	3750	6444	10747	12002	22587	45310	56728	52910	70705	75007	67527
Cap Spending $Mil	-832	-961	-1320	-1241	-3003	-7618	-10428	-8665	-11034	-12229	-12352
Free Cash Flow $Mil	2918	5483	9427	10761	19584	37692	46300	44245	59731	62778	55175

Profitability

	2006	2007	2008	2009	2010	2011	2012	2013	2014	2015	TTM
Return on Assets %	13.9	16.4	19.9	19.7	22.8	27.1	28.5	19.3	18.0	20.5	17.9
Return on Equity %	22.9	28.5	33.2	30.5	35.3	41.7	42.8	30.6	33.6	46.3	39.1
Asset Turnover	1.35	1.16	1.22	1.03	1.06	1.13	1.07	0.89	0.83	0.89	0.80
Net Margin %	10.3	14.2	16.3	19.2	21.5	24.0	26.7	21.7	21.6	22.9	22.3
Financial Leverage	1.7	1.7	1.6	1.5	1.6	1.5	1.5	1.7	2.1	2.4	2.3

Financial Health (USD)

	2006	2007	2008	2009	2010	2011	2012	2013	2014	2015	03-16
Long-Term Debt $Mil	—	—	—	—	—	—	0	16960	28987	53463	69374
Total Equity $Mil	9984	14532	22297	31640	47791	76615	118210	123549	111547	119355	130457
Debt/Equity	—	—	—	—	—	—	0.14	0.26	0.45	0.53	
Working Capital $Mil	8038	12657	18645	20049	20956	17018	19111	29628	5083	8768	19027

Valuation

	2006	2007	2008	2009	2010	2011	2012	2013	2014	2015	TTM
Price/Earnings	37.3	43.5	15.9	20.6	18.0	14.6	12.1	14.1	17.1	11.4	10.9
P/E vs. Market	—	0.0	0.0	0.0	0.0	—	0.0	0.0	0.0	0.0	0.6
Price/Sales	3.9	6.7	2.3	4.1	3.9	3.5	3.1	3.1	3.7	2.6	2.4
Price/Book	7.3	10.4	3.3	5.3	5.4	4.9	3.9	4.1	5.8	4.9	4.1
Price/Cash Flow	33.6	27.5	7.2	16.0	13.2	10.1	8.9	9.7	11.3	7.5	8.3

Quarterly Results (USD)

Revenue $Mil	Jun	Sep	Dec	Mar
Most Recent	49605.0	51501.0	75872.0	50557.0
Previous	37432.0	42123.0	74599.0	58010.0

Rev Growth %	Jun	Sep	Dec	Mar
Most Recent	32.5	22.3	1.7	-12.9
Previous	6.0	12.4	29.5	27.1

Earnings Per Share $	Jun	Sep	Dec	Mar
Most Recent	1.85	1.97	3.28	1.90
Previous	1.28	1.42	3.06	2.33

Close Competitors

	Mkt Cap $Mil	Rev $Mil	P/E	ROE%
Alphabet Inc C	509932	77988	31.3	14.2
Microsoft Corp	444667	86886	42.9	12.7

Major Fund Holders

	% of shares
Vanguard Total Stock Mkt Idx	1.89
Vanguard 500 Index Inv	1.31
AllianceBernstein US L/C Growth Eqty MF	0.00

5.4 Debt Investments (Bonds and Notes)

Bonds and notes are a form of debt issued by corporations and governments. When you buy a bond or a note, you are loaning money to that entity. The principal of the loan from you to the company or government entity (bond) is due on the maturity date of the bond. The yearly interest is paid to you by that entity. This regular interest payment is the reason investors put their money in bonds. The US Treasury issues bonds for terms longer than 10 years, and notes for terms between one year and 10 years. Treasury bills are issued for terms under one year.

Are Bonds and Notes Different?

Though these are both debt instruments that represent an obligation to pay, there are differences in how notes and bonds are constructed and viewed by regulatory agencies. For example, all bonds are considered securities, while notes may or may not be classified as securities. Securities are heavily regulated, so notes not classified as securities are subject to fewer rules.

Are Bonds and Notes Risky?

Bonds and notes are generally less risky than common stock, because bondholders can protect themselves with insurance and protective covenants, and they have a higher claim during a bankruptcy or liquidation procedure. But bondholders do experience risk: They are especially sensitive to interest rate risk and purchasing power risk. That's because of the relationship between the price of bonds and interest rates. These move in opposite directions: As the interest rate in the general market increases, bond prices will fall. The duration of a bond is a measure of this sensitivity. Bondholders receive a set interest rate, called the coupon, each year. Bonds of longer duration carry a higher interest rate because your money is tied up for a much longer period of time. Therefore, changes in the rate of inflation will affect the purchasing power of the bondholder.

How Do You Buy Bonds and Notes?

This is a tricky question! Individual bonds are bought over the counter (OTC), usually through a broker or registered representative. Ideally, you would diversify an investment portfolio by purchasing hundreds of different bonds. However, most people do not buy individual bonds. That's because each bond has a relatively large minimum transaction size ($10,000 to $25,000 per bond) and an associated transaction cost (commission paid to the broker). It's an efficient system for large investment accounts, but very inefficient or even impossible with smaller accounts. Therefore, most people purchase bonds inside of bond funds. These are professionally managed mutual funds that pool investors' money together and take advantage of diversification and efficiencies of scale. Smaller investors do not have as much protection against interest rate changes, and they don't benefit from the protective covenants that the individual bonds carry.

Reading Check

As a bondholder, do you own part of the company, or have you loaned the company money?

Fig 5.3 Brokerage Statement

An example of the interest rates offered that are dependent on the duration of a bond and the creditworthiness of the issuer of the bond.

Fixed Income Offerings										
									POWERED BY BondSource™	
	3 Mo	6 Mo	9 Mo	1 Yr	2 Yr	3 Yr	5 Yr	10 Yr	20 Yr	30 Yr+
CDs	0.55	0.70	0.70	0.90	1.15	1.35	1.65	1.95	3.36	--
Bonds										
U.S. Treasuries	0.34	0.55	0.65	0.76	0.86	0.97	1.28	1.69	2.08	2.40
U.S. Treasury Zeros	--	0.26	0.45	0.67	0.78	0.90	1.30	1.82	2.37	2.49
Government Agencies	--	0.45	0.55	0.83	1.09	1.25	1.65	2.15	2.78	3.44
Corporates (AAA)	--	--	--	0.76	1.13	1.18	1.62	2.50	3.42	3.96
Corporates (AA)	--	0.61	0.72	1.02	1.25	1.32	1.70	2.47	3.73	3.89
Corporates (A)		1.04	1.15	1.41	1.66	1.88	2.27	3.46	4.33	4.85
Municipals (AAA)	--	0.48	0.60	0.81	1.27	1.33	1.78	2.56	2.92	3.16
Municipals (AA)	--	0.46	0.69	2.02	1.45	2.06	2.97	3.73	3.95	4.10
Municipals (A)		0.74	0.73	2.02	1.69	2.06	3.02	4.08	4.02	4.10

Ratings by Standard & Poor's

5.5 Using Stocks and Bonds Together

Modern portfolio theory stresses the importance of owning assets that have little to no correlation. Simply put, mixing some investments that "zig" when others "zag" can make for a more stable portfolio. Stocks and bonds have been used together to this effect for decades. Other alternative investments include real estate, commodities, precious metals, and private equity. But as with individual bonds, it is hard for the individual investor to adequately diversify within these alternative sectors.

5.6 80/20, 60/40, 50/50

These ratios are examples of the typical mix of stocks and bonds in a portfolio. The first number is the stock holding, the second number is bonds and other types of fixed-income assets. This number is an oversimplification, but can provide some general idea about the makeup of a portfolio. Portfolio managers or mutual fund managers will usually state the ratio they work to maintain.

Reading Check

What is the appropriate mix of stocks and bonds in your own portfolio?

5.7 Using Assets to Create Income: Moving from the Accumulation Phase to the Distribution Phase

The average investor needs to accumulate retirement assets to replace the income they earned while working. During your years of working, you are contributing to your retirement accounts, purchasing other assets, and counting on the positive effects of compound interest. This focus on increasing the account balance can dominate the mind; it's a hard sentiment to shake off. But as you move from the accumulation phase to the distribution phase, generating consistent income to pay for necessities and other living expenses will take priority. Seeing a declining account balance each year is a hard pill to swallow. In today's environment, as interest rates continue to linger at historic lows, retirees are forced to use more and more principal each year to replace the income they're no longer earning.

That's why we invest in stocks, bonds, real estate, etc.: to accumulate assets that will provide us with income once we are no longer working.

5.8 Longevity

Are you going to outlive your money?

Everybody has basic living expenses: phone bills, groceries, utility bills, and rent or a mortgage. These are recurring expenses and are unavoidable for the rest of retirement. Having sufficient income to cover these expenses can mean the difference between a comfortable retirement and poverty.

Almost every retiree will receive a Social Security check, whether it is based on his or her own earnings record or that of another person. Social Security may or may not cover your expenses, but it will pay for the rest of your life. This recurring, consistent income can provide some security if you don't have an asset account balance.

An annuity can provide the same benefit; instead of being backed by the government, an annuity is backed by an insurance company. But unlike Social Security, some annuities will pay a lifetime benefit *and* provide a balance. Buying an immediate or a deferred annuity can protect you from outliving your money. An excellent tool for retirees is a fixed-index annuity. Moshe Milevsky, professor of finance and author of *Life Annuities: An Optimal Product for Retirement Income*, delves into the mathematics and behavioral science that show just how important an annuity is in a retiree's portfolio. The information that follows is derived from this book.

5.9 Fixed-Index Annuities: Downside Protection, Limited Upside

The most basic form of an annuity is an immediate annuity. The policyholder exchanges a lump sum of money for a series of payments from an insurance company; the cash balance of the annuity is $0. Immediate annuities pay a monthly benefit you cannot outlive, and some companies even offer inflation-adjusted payments. Once the annuity is purchased, the principal is invested by the insurance company. Any surplus returns are not returned to the policyholder or their beneficiaries; this is the limited upside of an annuity. The downside protection comes from the fact that your principal is guaranteed by the insurance company to never lose money.

A fixed-index annuity with a guaranteed lifetime withdrawal benefit rider (GLWB) can provide a benefit similar to an immediate annuity, but with a cash balance that participates in a rising market. These annuities are classified as deferred annuities; they are not in distribution (like an immediate annuity) and have a cash value. Once elected, lifetime benefits are paid under the guaranteed lifetime withdrawal benefit rider. That GLWB rider tracks the age of the owner or annuitant, and depending on when the owner elects to begin their benefit, a certain withdrawal benefit is locked in. Similar to Social Security, delaying this election will result in a higher lifetime payment. Older individuals will also have higher guaranteed withdrawal rates.

As withdrawals are made the cash balance of the annuity will decrease, but the annuity can earn interest annually. Fixed-index annuities offer a variety of interest options: The fixed-rate option pays a guaranteed interest rate for at least one year; indexed options will track common indexes like the S&P 500 or proprietary indexes, and credit a percentage of the growth in these indexes year after year. These interest payments can add to the principal of your annuity, increase guaranteed interest payments, and provide a larger legacy to your beneficiaries.

Fig 5.4 Immediate Annuity

This is an example of an immediate annuity that is purchasing an income for life.

OPTION ELECTED (IRREVOCABLE):	JOINT AND SURVIVOR, 10 YEAR MINIMUM FIXED PERIOD		
Maturity Value:	$46,513.36	Gross Payment Amount:	$302.74
Premium Tax (if applicable):	$0.00	Federal Income Tax:	10%
Net Maturity Value:	$46,531.36	State Income Tax:	0%
Payment Mode:	Monthly	Taxable Percentage:	100.00%
First Payment Date:	9/9/2016		
Payment Duration:	For your life and your joint payee's life only	Mailing Instructions: Direct electronic deposit	

Fig 5.5 Deferred Annuity with GLWB (Guaranteed Lifetime Withdrawal Benefit)

This is an example of a deferred annuity that can become an income for life at a future date.

Assumed Issue Date: April 27, 2016						
Assumes Initial Premium Amount of: $255,000						
					SINGLE LIFE LEVEL INCOME	
Deferral Years	Beginning of Year Age	End of Year Age	Income Base	Income Percentage	Guaranteed Lifetime Income Withdrawal	Annual Income if Confined *Must meet eligibility requirements
0	75	76	$293,250	6.00%	$17,595	$31,190*
1	76	77	$318,750	6.10%	$19,444	$38,888
2	77	78	$344,250	6.20%	$21,344	$42,687
3	78	79	$369,750	6.30%	$23,294	$46,589
4	79	80	$395,250	6.40%	$25,296	$50,592
5	80	81	$420,750	6.50%	$27,349	$54,698
6	81	82	$446,250	6.60%	$29,453	$58,905
7	82	83	$471,750	6.70%	$31,607	$63,215
8	83	84	$497,250	6.80%	$33,813	$37,626
9	84	85	$522,750	6.90%	$36,070	$72,140
10	85	86	$548,250	7.00%	$38,378	$76,755
11	86	87	$561,000	7.10%	$39,831	$79,662
12	87	88	$573,750	7.20%	$41,310	$82,620
13	88	89	$586,500	7.30%	$42,815	$85,629
14	89	90	$599,250	7.40%	$44,345	$88,689
15	90	91	$612,000	7.50%	$45,900	$91,800
20	95	96	$675,750	7.50%	$50,681	$101,363
25	100	101	$675,750	7.50%	$50,981	$101,363

This example assumes you have elected a single life income to start at age 80. In this example, the annual Lifetime Income Withdrawal you would receive is $27,349. Once started, the Lifetime Income Withdrawal amount is locked in assuming you do not take any excess withdrawals. Therefore you would continue to receive $27,349 in all subsequent years. Similarly, if the annuitant is confined to a qualified care facility and meets all eligibility requirements, assuming no excess withdrawals, the annual Lifetime Income Withdrawal amount is locked in once you commence Lifetime Income Withdrawals. Thus, if you are eligible at any point after the commencement of Lifetime Income Withdrawals, you would receive an annual Lifetime Income Withdrawal of $54,698.

5.10 Guaranteed Enhancements: Income for Long-Term Care Expenses

Though a fixed-index annuity can benefit from a rising market, it is also protected from a falling market. This is guaranteed and backed up by the claims-paying ability of the insurance company. Of course a rising market cannot be guaranteed, but some fixed-index annuities carry a guarantee to pay you an enhanced benefit if you are confined to a nursing home or are unable to complete at least two of the six activities of daily living (eating, dressing, bathing, transferring, toileting, and continence; for more on activities of daily living, see Module 3, page 30).

Having the money to pay for long-term care expenses is important, but having predictable income during retirement is just as important. A fixed-index annuity with these enhancements can provide both. Unlike traditional long-term care insurance, many of these annuities can be purchased without medical underwriting. The insurance company may ask you to attest that you are able to do all six activities of daily living. Or it may prevent you from electing the enhanced benefits payment for a few years after the annuity purchase.

5.11 How Should You Allocate Your Investments?

Our clients ask us all the time how they should allocate their investments. To answer the question, we conduct an important exercise: We ask our clients to fill out a risk tolerance questionnaire. The following quiz can help you quantify just how much risk you can stomach by posing different hypothetical scenarios and allowing you to pick the outcome or answer you feel best fits your own needs.

Fig 5.6 Risk Profile Questionnaire

Financials

What are your investment objectives?

- ❏ Receive current income (1)
- ❏ Invest for future retirement (3)
- ❏ Finance an education (2)
- ❏ Wealth accumulation (4)

What is your approximate net worth?
(Excluding your principal residence)

- ❏ Less than $50K (0)
- ❏ $500K-749K (0)
- ❏ $750K-999K (0)
- ❏ $50K-99K (0)
- ❏ $1M+ (0)
- ❏ $100K-249K (0)
- ❏ $250K-499K (0)

Time Horizon

For how many years will you be making the withdrawals?

- ❏ I plan to take a lump sum distribution (0)
- ❏ 4-6 years (3)
- ❏ 7-10 years (5)
- ❏ More than 10 years (8)
- ❏ 1-3 years (1)

How much do you rely on income from this investment?

- ❏ Heavily (0)
- ❏ Not at all (8)
- ❏ Moderately (2)
- ❏ Somewhat (4)

Your Risk Tolerance

How strongly do you agree or disagree with the following statement: "I am willing to lose larger sums of money in the short term if I can enjoy potentially higher returns in the long term."

- ❏ Strongly agree (8)
- ❏ Disagree (1)
- ❏ Agree (6)
- ❏ Strongly disagree (0)

Historically, markets have experienced downturns, both short-term and prolonged, followed by market recoveries. Suppose you owned a well-diversified portfolio that fell by 20% (i.e. $100,000 initial investment would now be worth $80,000) over a short period, consistent with the overall market. Assuming you still have 10 years until you begin withdrawals, how would you react?

- ❏ I would not change my portfolio (6)
- ❏ I would wait at least 1 year before changing to options that are more conservative (4)
- ❏ I would wait at least 3 months before changing to options that are more conservative (2)
- ❏ I would immediately change to options that are more conservative (0)

Which of the following statements best describes your attitude toward long-term investing?

- ❏ I am willing to accept the lower returns associated with conservative investments that have minimal chance for loss of principal (1)
- ❏ In order to pursue moderate returns, I am willing to accept moderate fluctuations in the value of my investments (3)
- ❏ In order to pursue moderately high returns, I am willing to accept significant fluctuations in the value of my investments (5)
- ❏ In seeking maximum returns, I am willing to accept large fluctuations in the value of my investments and substantial risk of loss to principal (8)

Describe the kind of risk you are comfortable with:

- ❏ I don't want to lose any money ever; I could handle only a very small loss over a few months at most (1)
- ❏ I could handle losses over one or two quarters, but would not be comfortable subjecting myself to longer down periods (2)
- ❏ I could handle a one-year loss, but do not want to pursue a strategy that could result in longer periods of loss (3)
- ❏ I could handle being down over a three-year period, but not longer (5)
- ❏ I could accept being down over longer than three years if my long-term return potential was above average (7)

5.12 How Are Your Investments Allocated Now?

After working through the risk tolerance questionnaire, we use Morningstar®'s research to analyze your current portfolio and compare it to your personal risk tolerance. We often see a big difference between the actual risk in our clients' portfolios and their self-reported risk tolerance scores. It is especially important to create a plan if the risk tolerance doesn't match the investments. Even if the match is good, as you transition into retirement you should review your portfolio's ability to create retirement income. Risk tolerance is only one part of the retirement plan.

Fig 5.7 Morningstar® Portfolio Snapshot

This is an assessment of the risk a client is taking in their portfolio and the returns they have received based upon that risk.

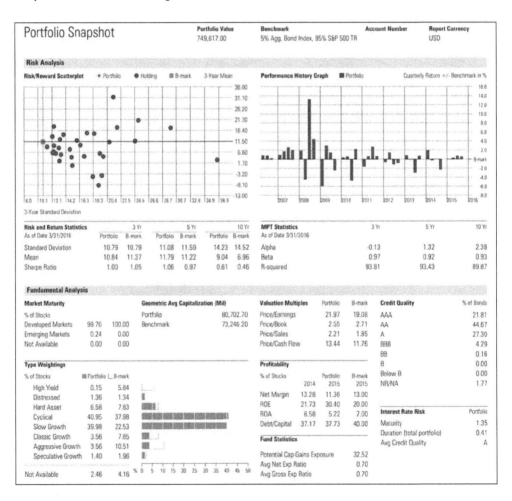

Portfolio Snapshot

Portfolio Value	749,617.00
Benchmark	5% Agg. Bond Index, 95% S&P 500 TR
Account Number	
Report Currency	USD

Analysis

Asset Allocation

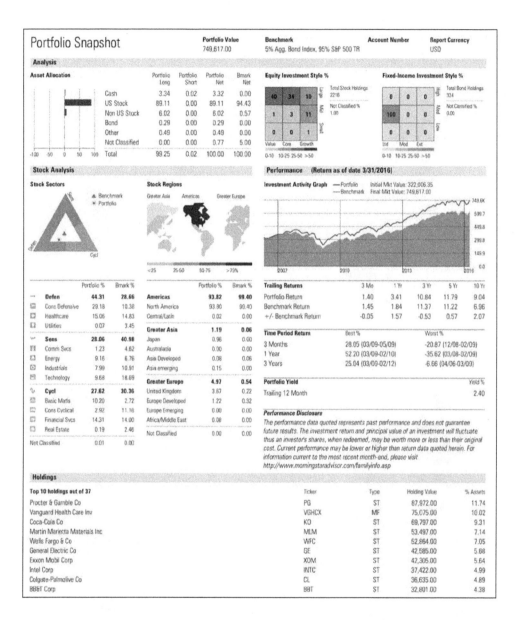

	Portfolio Long	Portfolio Short	Portfolio Net	Bmark Net
Cash	3.34	0.02	3.32	0.00
US Stock	89.11	0.00	89.11	94.43
Non US Stock	6.02	0.00	6.02	0.57
Bond	0.29	0.00	0.29	0.00
Other	0.49	0.00	0.49	0.00
Not Classified	0.00	0.00	0.77	5.00
Total	99.25	0.02	100.00	100.00

Equity Investment Style %

Total Stock Holdings 2216
Not Classified % 1.00

40	34	10
1	3	11
0	0	1

Value / Core / Growth
0-10 10-25 25-50 >50

Fixed-Income Investment Style %

Total Bond Holdings 324
Not Classified % 0.00

0	0	0
100	0	0
0	0	0

Ltd / Mod / Ext
0-10 10-25 25-50 >50

Stock Analysis

Stock Sectors

▲ Benchmark
● Portfolio

Stock Regions

<25 25-50 50-75 >75%

		Portfolio %	Bmark %
--	**Defen**	**44.31**	**28.66**
	Cons Defensive	29.18	10.38
	Healthcare	15.06	14.83
	Utilities	0.07	3.45
~	**Sens**	**28.06**	**40.98**
	Comm Svcs	1.23	4.62
	Energy	9.16	6.76
	Industrials	7.99	10.91
	Technology	9.68	18.69
⟳	**Cycl**	**27.62**	**30.36**
	Basic Matls	10.20	2.72
	Cons Cyclical	2.92	11.16
	Financial Svcs	14.31	14.00
	Real Estate	0.19	2.46
	Not Classified	0.01	0.00

	Portfolio %	Bmark %
Americas	**93.82**	**99.40**
North America	93.80	99.40
Central/Latin	0.02	0.00
Greater Asia	**1.19**	**0.06**
Japan	0.96	0.00
Australasia	0.00	0.00
Asia Developed	0.08	0.06
Asia emerging	0.15	0.00
Greater Europe	**4.97**	**0.54**
United Kingdom	3.67	0.22
Europe Developed	1.22	0.32
Europe Emerging	0.00	0.00
Africa/Middle East	0.08	0.00
Not Classified	0.00	0.00

Performance (Return as of date 3/31/2016)

Investment Activity Graph — Portfolio — Benchmark
Initial Mkt Value: 322,006.35
Final Mkt Value: 749,617.00

749.6K
599.7
449.8
299.8
149.9
0.0

2007   2010   2013   2016

Trailing Returns

	3 Mo	1 Yr	3 Yr	5 Yr	10 Yr
Portfolio Return	1.40	3.41	10.84	11.79	9.04
Benchmark Return	1.45	1.84	11.37	11.22	6.96
+/- Benchmark Return	-0.05	1.57	-0.53	0.57	2.07

Time Period Return	Best %	Worst %
3 Months	28.05 (03/09-05/09)	-20.87 (12/08-02/09)
1 Year	52.20 (03/09-02/10)	-35.62 (03/08-02/09)
3 Years	25.04 (03/09-02/12)	-6.66 (04/06-03/09)

Portfolio Yield	Yield %
Trailing 12 Month	2.40

Performance Disclosure

The performance data quoted represents past performance and does not guarantee future results. The investment return and principal value of an investment will fluctuate thus an investor's shares, when redeemed, may be worth more or less than their original cost. Current performance may be lower or higher than return data quoted herein. For information current to the most recent month-end, please visit http://www.morningstaradvisor.com/familyinfo.asp

Holdings

Top 10 holdings out of 37

	Ticker	Type	Holding Value	% Assets
Procter & Gamble Co	PG	ST	87,972.00	11.74
Vanguard Health Care Inv	VGHCX	MF	75,075.00	10.02
Coca-Cola Co	KO	ST	69,797.00	9.31
Martin Marietta Materials Inc	MLM	ST	53,497.00	7.14
Wells Fargo & Co	WFC	ST	52,864.00	7.05
General Electric Co	GE	ST	42,585.00	5.68
Exxon Mobil Corp	XOM	ST	42,305.00	5.64
Intel Corp	INTC	ST	37,422.00	4.99
Colgate-Palmolive Co	CL	ST	36,635.00	4.89
BB&T Corp	BBT	ST	32,801.00	4.38

5.13 A Safe Withdrawal Rate: The Trinity Study

The Trinity Study is a famous and often-referenced study conducted by finance professors at Trinity University. Their research has been used to build the "4% withdrawal rate rule of thumb." After studying data from 1925 to 1995, the professors concluded that a 3% to 4% withdrawal rate is extremely unlikely to exhaust a portfolio over 15 to 30 years.

The authors caution that these observations can be used to help plan a distribution strategy, but should not be considered a "matter of contract." The real world is a different place; picking a withdrawal rate and asset allocation will not guarantee that your own assets will outlive your own life. Mid-course plan corrections and lifetime annuities will help create a more secure retirement.

Reading Check

What is your plan to draw down or live off of your investments in retirement?

INVESTMENT PLANNER

List all non-qualified accounts (those not listed in Module 4), such as bank accounts, CDs, brokerage accounts, life insurance with cash value, etc. To prepare, gather statements from these accounts.

Institution	Stocks, Bonds, Cash Value Combination	Balance

Complete the Risk Profile Questionnaire on page 81 (jointly if you are married).

LIFE INSURANCE AND ESTATE PLANNING

KEY QUESTIONS

- What is the purpose of life insurance?

- Are there different kinds of life insurance?

- What is estate planning?

- Why is it important to always update beneficiary designations?

- What are the four main documents that need to be prepared for estate planning?

- How do federal estate taxes affect estate planning?

Corresponds to Chapter 7, "Life Insurance, Estate Planning, and Your Legacy,"
*in **The Complete Cardinal Guide.***

6.1 Types of Life Insurance

The purpose of owning life insurance in retirement is to create immediate funds for your survivors to pay for final expenses. The examples below are based on $25,000 of life insurance, which is a minimum amount to cover final expenses. If you have a large estate, or longer-term income needs for survivors, gifting, or charity, then you may need a substantially greater amount of life insurance.

Funeral*	$10,000
Attorney Fees for Estate Settlement	$2,000
Executor	$1,000
6–12 Months Income Replacement	$12,000
	$25,000

National median price of a funeral in 2014 was $8,517 (National Funeral Directors Association).

Example 1

Example 1 has a $25,000 death benefit with full underwriting, which means the life insurance company will examine you from head to toe. At these rates, you are allowed to have some minor health issues. If you have significant health conditions, they will charge you more or possibly turn you down for the policy.

Fig 6.1

Female • Nonsmoker • Full Underwriting • Death Benefit: $25,000

Age 55	Age 70
ANNUAL PREMIUM	ANNUAL PREMIUM
$488	$1,079

Example 2

Example 2 is the same as Example 1, but with higher premiums because there is no head-to-toe exam. Simplified underwriting means the life insurance company will ask you some limited health questions and issue the policy if you pass.

Fig 6.2

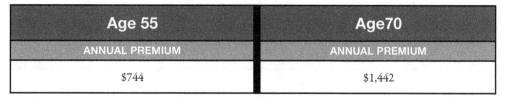

Female • Nonsmoker • Simplified Underwriting • Benefit: $25,000

Age 55	Age70
ANNUAL PREMIUM	ANNUAL PREMIUM
$744	$1,442

Example 3

Example 3 is life insurance available to anyone, ages 50 to 85, regardless of their health. We have written these policies on people with cancer, kidney dialysis, heart disease...you name it. The policy is more expensive (see below) and has limited benefits during the first two years it is in force.

Fig 6.3

Female • Can Smoke • No Underwriting • Benefit: $25,000

Age 55	Age70
ANNUAL PREMIUM	ANNUAL PREMIUM
$1,059	$2,046

During the first two policy years, the benefit payment for death due to any reason other than accident is a full refund of all premiums paid plus 10% interest. If death is due to accidental reasons, the full face amount is paid.

Example 4

Example 4 is for people who do not want to pay premiums monthly or yearly. One single premium is paid in the beginning and the policy pays $25,000 at your death. The health underwriting is a few simple questions—no exam!

Fig 6.4

Female • Nonsmoker • Simplified Underwriting • Benefit: $25,000

Age 55	Age 70
SINGLE PREMIUM	SINGLE PREMIUM
$10,593	$15,432

This single-premium policy allows you to access the $25,000 death benefit to pay for long-term care while you're still alive.

Reading Check

What are some of the different kinds of life insurance policies that are available to consumers? What are the differences between them?

6.2 Beneficiary Designations

Below is a sample beneficiary form from a life insurance company. A Primary beneficiary is first in line. A Contingent beneficiary gets paid if the primary beneficiary is already deceased when the policy pays its benefit.

Fig 6.5

5. Beneficiary (P - Primary, C - Contingent)

If the beneficiary listed below is not designated as Primary or Contingent beneficiary, it will automatically default to a Primary designation. All shares will be divided equally unless otherwise noted in the space provided.

A joint owner will be the sole Primary Beneficiary, notwithstanding any designation made below.

List additional beneficiaries on the Additional Beneficiary Designation Form. Share/Percentage must equal 100%. If beneficiary is a trust, list the name of the trust, name(s) of the current trustee(s), and trust agreement date **AND provide either a notarized trust certification or copies of the first page and signature page of the trust.**

If the owner of the contract applied for is a trust, the trust must be designated as the sole Primary Beneficiary.

The owner agrees that, in the event that the owner should die before the annuity contract is issued, this designation shall be treated as a transfer on death designation for any funds properly received by the Company intended for this annuity contract. Accordingly, it is agreed that the Company will pay such funds to the joint owner, or if none, then to the person(s) designated as beneficiary below.

❏ P ❏ C Share/Percentage .... %	❏ P ❏ C Share/Percentage ....%
Name..	Name..
Address	Address ....
....	....
Country....................Phone..........	Country....................Phone..........
E-mail address.................................	E-mail address.................................
SSN....................Birth date...........	SSN....................Birth date...........
Relationship....................................	Relationship....................................
❏ P ❏ C Share/Percentage ....%	❏ P ❏ C Share/Percentage ....%
Name..	Name..
Address	Address ....
....	....
Country....................Phone..........	Country....................Phone..........
E-mail address.................................	E-mail address.................................
SSN....................Birth date...........	SSN....................Birth date...........
Relationship....................................	Relationship....................................

"Per Stirpes" means if one of the beneficiaries dies before the insured, that beneficiary's share will pass to their descendants.

"Per Capita" means if one or more of the beneficiaries dies before the insured, the death benefit is divided between the remaining beneficiaries.

6.3 Estate Planning Documents

Everyone should prepare four key estate planning documents: last will and testament; health-care power of attorney; general durable power of attorney; and HIPAA release. Having these documents in order before you die will make life easier for your heirs and minimize their expenses.

6.3.1 Last Will and Testament

Below is a will brought to us by one of our clients. It was made in Arizona but is still good in North Carolina. It is presented here as an example.

Fig 6.6

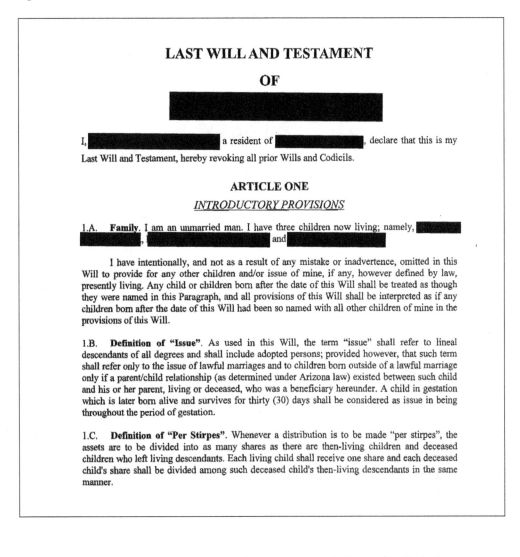

LAST WILL AND TESTAMENT

OF

I, _____ a resident of _____, declare that this is my Last Will and Testament, hereby revoking all prior Wills and Codicils.

ARTICLE ONE

INTRODUCTORY PROVISIONS

1.A.   **Family.** I am an unmarried man. I have three children now living; namely, _____ , _____ and _____

I have intentionally, and not as a result of any mistake or inadvertence, omitted in this Will to provide for any other children and/or issue of mine, if any, however defined by law, presently living. Any child or children born after the date of this Will shall be treated as though they were named in this Paragraph, and all provisions of this Will shall be interpreted as if any children born after the date of this Will had been so named with all other children of mine in the provisions of this Will.

1.B.   **Definition of "Issue".** As used in this Will, the term "issue" shall refer to lineal descendants of all degrees and shall include adopted persons; provided however, that such term shall refer only to the issue of lawful marriages and to children born outside of a lawful marriage only if a parent/child relationship (as determined under Arizona law) existed between such child and his or her parent, living or deceased, who was a beneficiary hereunder. A child in gestation which is later born alive and survives for thirty (30) days shall be considered as issue in being throughout the period of gestation.

1.C.   **Definition of "Per Stirpes".** Whenever a distribution is to be made "per stirpes", the assets are to be divided into as many shares as there are then-living children and deceased children who left living descendants. Each living child shall receive one share and each deceased child's share shall be divided among such deceased child's then-living descendants in the same manner.

ARTICLE TWO

NOMINATION OF FIDUCIARIES

2.A. **Personal Representatives.** I nominate my son ███████████████ as Personal Representative of my Will. If he shall fail to qualify or shall cease to act, I nominate my son ████████████ as successor Personal Representative.

2.B. **Appointment of Special Personal Representative.** If for any reason my Personal Representative is unwilling or unable to act as Personal Representative with respect to any provision of my Will or the administration of my Estate, my Personal Representative shall appoint, in writing, an individual, a bank, or a trust company that is not related or subordinate to my Personal Representative within the meaning of §672(c) of the Internal Revenue Code (hereinafter referred to as "the Code") to act as a substitute or special Personal Representative for such purpose, and may revoke any such appointment at will. Each substitute or special Personal Representative so acting shall exercise all administrative and fiduciary powers granted by my Will unless expressly limited by the delegating Personal Representative in the instrument appointing such substitute or special Personal Representative. Any substitute or special Personal Representative may resign at any time by delivering written notice to my Personal Representative to that effect.

2.C. **No Bond Required.** Any fiduciary appointed under this Article Two shall serve without bond being required.

ARTICLE THREE

DISTRIBUTION PROVISIONS

3.A. **Payment of Estate Expenses.** My Personal Representative may pay from my Estate all debts which are then due and enforceable against my Estate, the expenses of my last illness, the expenses of my final disposition without the necessity of prior court approval, the expenses of administering my Estate, and all death taxes and governmental charges imposed upon and made payable from my Estate under the laws of the United States or of any state or country by reason of my death.

3.B. **Tangible Personal Property.** I give my tangible personal property to my sons in equal shares. I direct that all costs of safeguarding, insuring, storing and delivering my tangible personal property to the beneficiaries entitled thereto be paid out of my estate as an expense of administration.

3.C. **Distribution At My Death.** I give the remainder of my Estate to my then-living issue, per stirpes. If a beneficiary has not yet attained the age of twenty-one (21), this distribution shall be held for such beneficiary in a custodial account under the provisions of the Arizona Uniform Transfer to Minors Act with the parent of such beneficiary as the custodian.

ARTICLE FOUR

ESTATE ADMINISTRATION

4.A. **General Powers of Personal Representative.** Subject to any limitations stated elsewhere in this Will, my Personal Representative shall have, in addition to all of the powers now or hereafter conferred on my Personal Representative by Title 14 of the Arizona Revised Statutes, and any powers enumerated elsewhere in this Will, the power to perform any of the acts specified in this section without the necessity of court approval:

(1)   To take possession or control of all of my Estate subject to disposition by this Will, and collect all debts due to me or to my Estate;

(2)   To receive the rents, issues, and profits from all real and personal property in my Estate until the estate is settled or delivered over by order of court to my heirs or beneficiaries;

(3)   To pay taxes on, and take all steps reasonably necessary for the management, protection, and preservation of, all property in my Estate;

(4)   To insure the property of my Estate against damage or loss, and insure my Personal Representative against liability to third persons;

(5)   To deposit money belonging to my Estate in an insured account in a financial institution in Arizona;

(6)   If any asset of my Estate consists of an option right, to exercise the option and to use any funds or property in my Estate to acquire the property covered by the option;

(7)   To hold any securities or other property, both real and personal, in the name of my Personal Representative, in the name of such nominee as my Personal Representative shall select, or in the form of "street certificates," without in any of such cases disclosing the fact that such property is held in a fiduciary capacity, and to indemnify any such nominee against any loss resulting from holding such property as nominee;

(8)   To vote in person, and give proxies to exercise, any voting rights with respect to any stock, any membership in a nonprofit corporation, or any other property in my Estate, and waive notice of a meeting, give consent to the holding of a meeting, and authorize, ratify, approve, or confirm any action that could be taken by shareholders, members, or property owners;

(9)   To make any elections permitted under any pension, profit sharing, employee stock ownership or other benefit plan;

(10)   To disclaim or renounce, in whole or in part or with respect to specific amounts, parts, fractional shares or assets, any legacy, devise, or interest in or privilege or power over any trust or other disposition provided for my benefit under the Will or other instrument of any person at any time within nine months after the date of the transfer (whether by reason of such person's death or otherwise) which created an interest in me or my Estate;

(11)   To sell and to grant options to purchase all or any part of my Estate, both real and personal, at any time, at public or private sale, for such consideration, whether or not the highest possible consideration, and upon such terms, including credit, as my Personal Representative shall deem advisable, and to execute, acknowledge and deliver deeds or other instruments in connection therewith. No purchaser shall be held to see to the application of the purchase money;

(12)   To lease any real estate for such term or terms and upon such provisions and conditions as my Personal Representative shall deem advisable, including the granting of options to renew, options to extend the term or terms, and options to purchase;

(13)   To borrow and to pledge or mortgage any property as collateral, and to make secured or unsecured loans. My Personal Representative is specifically authorized to make loans without interest to any beneficiary hereunder. No individual or entity loaning property to my Personal Representative shall be held to see to the application of such property;

(14)   To pay any and all charges reasonably incurred in connection with or incidental to the distribution of any property of my Estate, including but not limited to expenses of storage, freight, shipping, delivery, packing, and insurance; and, on any accounting, treat any such expenditures as expenses of the administration of my Estate;

(15)   To dispose of or abandon tangible personal property (including donation to any charitable organization or organizations of my Personal Representative's choice), except tangible personal property that is a specific gift, when the cost of collecting, maintaining, and safeguarding the property would exceed its fair market value;

(16)   To commence and prosecute, either individually or jointly with my heirs or beneficiaries, any action necessary or proper to quiet title to or recover possession of any real or personal property in my Estate; and,

(17)   To employ others in connection with the administration of my Estate, including legal counsel, investment advisors, brokers, accountants and agents, notwithstanding the fact that my Personal Representative may receive a direct or indirect financial benefit as a result of such employment or may otherwise be affiliated with any of them, and to pay reasonable compensation thereto in addition to that to be paid to my Personal Representative.

4.B. **Power to Invest.** To retain for whatever period my Personal Representative shall deem advisable any property, including property owned by me at my death, and to invest and reinvest any money of my Estate not reasonably required for the immediate administration of my Estate in any kind of property, real, personal, or mixed, and in any kind of investment, including but not limited to improved and unimproved real property, interest-bearing accounts, certificates of deposit, corporate and governmental obligations of any kind, preferred or common stocks, mutual funds (including mutual funds of the "load" and "no load" variety), investment trusts, money-market funds, taxable and tax-exempt commercial paper, repurchase and reverse repurchase agreements, and stocks, obligations, and shares or units of common trust funds of any corporate fiduciary; regardless of whether any particular investment would be proper for the Personal Representative and regardless of the extent of diversification of the assets held hereunder.

4.C. **Power to Make Tax Elections.** To the extent permitted by law, and without regard to the resulting effect on any other provision of this Will, on any person interested in my Estate, or on the amount of taxes that may be payable, my Personal Representative shall have the power to choose a valuation date for tax purposes; choose the methods to pay any death taxes; elect to treat or use any item for state or federal estate or income tax purposes as an income tax deduction or an estate tax deduction; and, to disclaim all or any portion of any interest in property passing at or after my death to my Estate or to a trust created by me or established for my benefit.

4.D. **Division or Distribution in Cash or in Kind.** In order to satisfy a pecuniary gift or to distribute or divide estate assets into shares or partial shares, my Personal Representative may distribute or divide those assets in kind, or divide undivided interests in those assets, or sell all or any part of those assets and distribute or divide the property in cash, in kind, or partly in cash and partly in kind, with or without regard to tax basis. Property distributed to satisfy a pecuniary gift under this Will shall be valued at its fair market value at the time of distribution.

4.E. **Digital Assets.** My Personal Representative shall have the power to access, manage, and control any and all forms of digital assets, accounts and rights in which I have an interest at my death;

4.F. **Special Distributions Options.** If any income and/or principal of my Estate hereunder ever vests outright under the provisions of this Will in a person not yet twenty-one (21), or a person who suffers from substance abuse, or a person who my Personal Representative determines is incapacitated, or a person whose financial circumstances are such that failure to delay distributions will actually reduce the benefits to such person, then my Personal Representative, in my Personal Representative's discretion and without supervision of any court, shall hold or distribute such income and/or principal (subsequently referred to in this Paragraph as the "protected property") in accordance with the following provisions:

    (1)   My Personal Representative may distribute any protected property to or for the benefit of such beneficiary: (a) directly to the beneficiary; (b) on behalf of the beneficiary for the beneficiary's exclusive benefit; (c) to any account in a bank, credit union, mutual fund and/or brokerage firm either in the name of such beneficiary or in a form reserving title, management and custody of such account to a suitable person for the use of such beneficiary (such as an account created under the Uniform Gifts to Minors Act or Uniform Transfers to Minors Act of any state); (d) in any form of an annuity; and, (e) in all ways provided by law dealing with gifts or distributions to or for minors or persons under incapacity. The receipt for distributions by any such person shall fully discharge my Personal Representative.

(2)   In determining whether to make distributions, my Personal Representative may consider other resources of the beneficiary, any governmental entitlements and the future needs of the beneficiary. The protected property shall, at all times, remain free of all claims by any governmental agency and/or creditors of the beneficiary.

(3)   Notwithstanding the provisions of the preceding subparagraphs or any other provision of this Agreement, my Personal Representative shall not suspend any mandatory distributions required for a trust to qualify, in whole or in part, for any Federal or state charitable deduction.

4.G.   **Liability**. Unless due to such Personal Representative's own willful default or gross negligence, no Personal Representative shall be liable for such Personal Representative's acts or omissions nor those of any co-Personal Representative or prior Personal Representative.

4.H.   **Court Supervision**. My Estate may be managed, administered, distributed, and settled without Court supervision to the maximum extent permissible by law.

ARTICLE FIVE

CONCLUDING PROVISIONS

5.A.   **Definition of Death Taxes**. The term "death taxes" as used in this Will shall mean all inheritance, estate, succession, and other similar taxes that are payable by any person on account of that person's interest in my Estate or by reason of my death, including penalties and interest, but excluding any additional tax that may be assessed under Internal Revenue Code §2032A.

5.B.   **Payment of Death Taxes**. Death taxes shall be prorated and apportioned among the persons interested in that property as provided by the laws of the State of Arizona, whether or not such property is inventoried in my probate estate.

5.C.   **Period of Survivorship**. For the purposes of this Will, a beneficiary shall not be deemed to have survived me if that beneficiary dies within three (3) months after my death.

5.D.   **Guardian Ad Litem**. I direct that the representation by a guardian ad litem of the interests of persons unborn, unascertained, or legally incompetent to act in proceedings for the allowance of accounts hereunder be dispensed with to the extent permitted by law.

5.E.   **Beneficial Interests**. The interest of any beneficiary in any share or part of this Will, both as to principal and income, shall not be alienable, assignable, attachable, transferable nor paid by way of anticipation, nor in compliance with any order, assignment or covenant and shall not be applied to, or held liable for, any of their debts or obligations either in law or equity and shall not in any event pass to his, her or their assignee under any instrument or under any insolvency or bankruptcy law, and shall not be subject to the interference or control of creditors, spouses or others.

5.F.   **Captions**. The captions appearing in this Will are for convenience of reference only, and shall be disregarded in determining the meaning and effect of the provisions of this Will.

5.G.   **Severability Clause**. If any provision of this Will is invalid, that provision shall be disregarded, and the remainder of this Will shall be construed as if the invalid provision had not been included.

5.H.   **Governing Law**. All questions concerning the validity and interpretation of this Will shall be governed by Title 14 of the Arizona Revised Statutes.

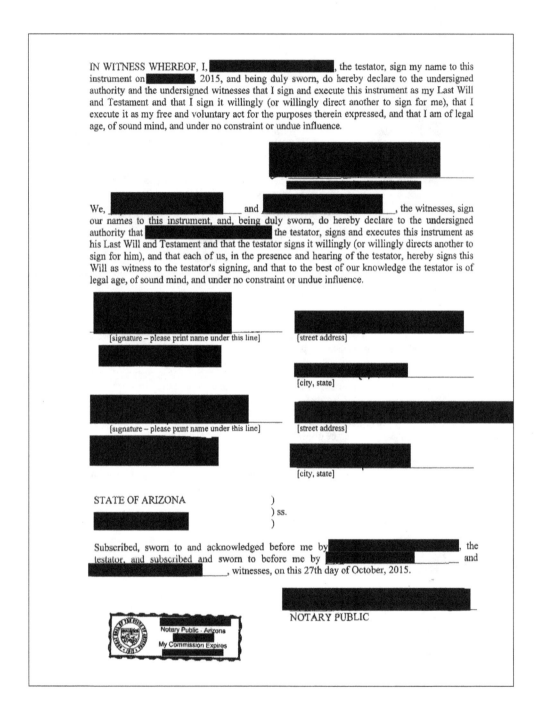

IN WITNESS WHEREOF, I, ▮▮▮▮▮▮▮▮▮▮▮▮, the testator, sign my name to this instrument on ▮▮▮▮▮, 2015, and being duly sworn, do hereby declare to the undersigned authority and the undersigned witnesses that I sign and execute this instrument as my Last Will and Testament and that I sign it willingly (or willingly direct another to sign for me), that I execute it as my free and voluntary act for the purposes therein expressed, and that I am of legal age, of sound mind, and under no constraint or undue influence.

We, ▮▮▮▮▮▮▮▮▮▮ and ▮▮▮▮▮▮▮▮▮▮, the witnesses, sign our names to this instrument, and, being duly sworn, do hereby declare to the undersigned authority that ▮▮▮▮▮▮▮▮▮▮ the testator, signs and executes this instrument as his Last Will and Testament and that the testator signs it willingly (or willingly directs another to sign for him), and that each of us, in the presence and hearing of the testator, hereby signs this Will as witness to the testator's signing, and that to the best of our knowledge the testator is of legal age, of sound mind, and under no constraint or undue influence.

_____
[signature – please print name under this line]

_____
[street address]

_____
[city, state]

_____
[signature – please print name under this line]

_____
[street address]

_____
[city, state]

STATE OF ARIZONA)
) ss.
▮▮▮▮▮▮▮▮)

Subscribed, sworn to and acknowledged before me by ▮▮▮▮▮▮▮▮, the testator, and subscribed and sworn to before me by ▮▮▮▮▮▮▮▮ and ▮▮▮▮▮▮▮▮, witnesses, on this 27th day of October, 2015.

Notary Public - Arizona
My Commission Expires

_____
NOTARY PUBLIC

6.3.2 Health-Care Power of Attorney

A health-care power of attorney is necessary so your loved ones can make health-care decisions for you when you can't.

Fig 6.7

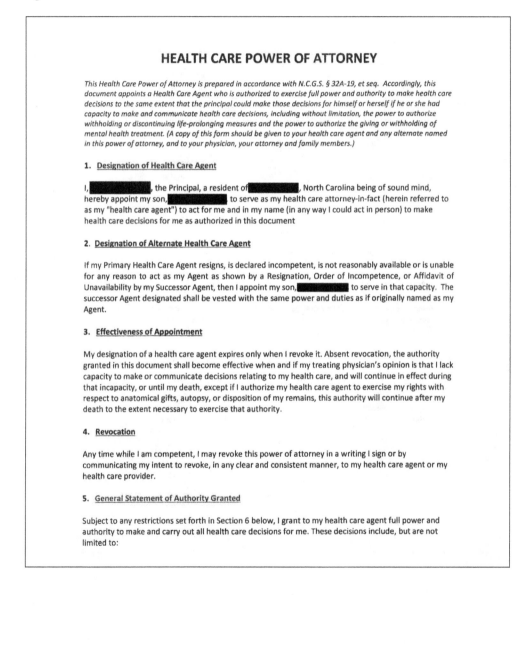

HEALTH CARE POWER OF ATTORNEY

This Health Care Power of Attorney is prepared in accordance with N.C.G.S. § 32A-19, et seq. Accordingly, this document appoints a Health Care Agent who is authorized to exercise full power and authority to make health care decisions to the same extent that the principal could make those decisions for himself or herself if he or she had capacity to make and communicate health care decisions, including without limitation, the power to authorize withholding or discontinuing life-prolonging measures and the power to authorize the giving or withholding of mental health treatment. (A copy of this form should be given to your health care agent and any alternate named in this power of attorney, and to your physician, your attorney and family members.)

1. Designation of Health Care Agent

I, ▮▮▮▮▮▮, the Principal, a resident of ▮▮▮▮▮▮, North Carolina being of sound mind, hereby appoint my son, ▮▮▮▮▮▮ to serve as my health care attorney-in-fact (herein referred to as my "health care agent") to act for me and in my name (in any way I could act in person) to make health care decisions for me as authorized in this document

2. Designation of Alternate Health Care Agent

If my Primary Health Care Agent resigns, is declared incompetent, is not reasonably available or is unable for any reason to act as my Agent as shown by a Resignation, Order of Incompetence, or Affidavit of Unavailability by my Successor Agent, then I appoint my son, ▮▮▮▮▮▮ to serve in that capacity. The successor Agent designated shall be vested with the same power and duties as if originally named as my Agent.

3. Effectiveness of Appointment

My designation of a health care agent expires only when I revoke it. Absent revocation, the authority granted in this document shall become effective when and if my treating physician's opinion is that I lack capacity to make or communicate decisions relating to my health care, and will continue in effect during that incapacity, or until my death, except if I authorize my health care agent to exercise my rights with respect to anatomical gifts, autopsy, or disposition of my remains, this authority will continue after my death to the extent necessary to exercise that authority.

4. Revocation

Any time while I am competent, I may revoke this power of attorney in a writing I sign or by communicating my intent to revoke, in any clear and consistent manner, to my health care agent or my health care provider.

5. General Statement of Authority Granted

Subject to any restrictions set forth in Section 6 below, I grant to my health care agent full power and authority to make and carry out all health care decisions for me. These decisions include, but are not limited to:

A. Requesting, reviewing, and receiving any information, verbal or written, regarding my physical or mental health, including, but not limited to, medical and hospital records, and to consent to the disclosure of this information.

B. Employing or discharging my health care providers.

C. Consenting to and authorizing my admission to and discharge from a hospital, nursing or convalescent home, hospice, long-term care facility, or other health care facility.

D. Consenting to and authorizing my admission to and retention in a facility for the care or treatment of mental illness.

E. Consenting to and authorizing the administration of medications for mental health treatment and electroconvulsive treatment (ECT) commonly referred to as "shock treatment."

F. Giving consent for, withdrawing consent for, or withholding consent for, X-ray, anesthesia, medication, surgery, and all other diagnostic and treatment procedures ordered by or under the authorization of a licensed physician, dentist, podiatrist, or other health care provider. This authorization specifically includes the power to consent to measures for relief of pain.

G. Authorizing the withholding or withdrawal of life-prolonging measures.

H. Providing my medical information at the request of any individual acting as my attorney-in-fact under a durable power of attorney or as a Trustee or successor Trustee under any Trust Agreement of which I am a Grantor or Trustee, or at the request of any other individual whom my health care agent believes should have such information. I desire that such information be provided whenever it would expedite the prompt and proper handling of my affairs or the affairs of any person or entity for which I have some responsibility. In addition, I authorize my health care agent to take any and all legal steps necessary to ensure compliance with my instructions providing access to my protected health information. Such steps shall include resorting to any and all legal procedures in and out of courts as may be necessary to enforce my rights under the law and shall include attempting to recover attorneys' fees against anyone who does not comply with this health care power of attorney.

I. To the extent I have not already made valid and enforceable arrangements during my lifetime that have not been revoked, exercising any right I may have to authorize an autopsy or direct the disposition of my remains.

J. Taking any lawful actions that may be necessary to carry out these decisions, including, but not limited to: (i) signing, executing, delivering, and acknowledging any agreement, release, authorization, or other document that may be necessary, desirable, convenient, or proper in order to exercise and carry out any of these powers; (ii) granting releases of liability to medical providers or others; and (iii) incurring reasonable costs on my behalf related to exercising these powers, provided that this health care power of attorney shall not give my health care agent general authority over my property or financial affairs.

6. Guardianship Provision

If it becomes necessary for a court to appoint a guardian of my person, I nominate the persons designated in Section 1, in the order named, to be the guardian of my person, to serve without bond or security. The guardian shall act consistently with G.S. 35A-1201(a)(5).

7. Reliance of Third Parties on Health Care Agent

A. No person who relies in good faith upon the authority of or any representations by my health care agent shall be liable to me, my estate, my heirs, successors, assigns, or personal representatives, for actions or omissions in reliance on that authority or those representations.

B. The powers conferred on my health care agent by this document may be exercised by my health care agent alone, and my health care agent's signature or action taken under the authority granted in this document may be accepted by persons as fully authorized by me and with the same force and effect as if I were personally present, competent, and acting on my own behalf. All acts performed in good faith by my health care agent pursuant to this power of attorney are done with my consent and shall have the same validity and effect as if I were present and exercised the powers myself, and shall inure to the benefit of and bind me, my estate, my heirs, successors, assigns, and personal representatives. The authority of my health care agent pursuant to this power of attorney shall be superior to and binding upon my family, relatives, friends, and others.

8. HIPAA Release Authority

I intend for my agent to be treated as I would be with respect to my rights regarding the use and disclosure of my individually identifiable health information or other medical records. This release authority applies to any information governed by the Health Insurance Portability and Accountability Act of 1996 (aka HIPAA), 42 USC 1320d and 45 CFR 160-164.

I authorize: any physician, health-care professional, dentist, health plan, hospital, clinic, laboratory, pharmacy or other covered health-care provider, any insurance company and the Medical Information Bureau Inc. or other health-care clearinghouse that has provided treatment or services to me, or that has paid for or is seeking payment from me for such services, to give, disclose and release to my agent, without restriction, all of my individually identifiable health information and medical records regarding any past , present or future medical or mental health condition, including all information relating to the diagnosis and treatment of HIV/AIDS, sexually transmitted diseases, mental illness, and drug or alcohol abuse.

The authority given my agent shall supersede any prior agreement that I may have made with my health-care providers to restrict access to or disclosure of my individually identifiable health information. The authority given my agent has no expiration date and shall expire only in the event that I revoke the authority in writing and deliver it to my health-care provider.

9. Miscellaneous Provisions

A.   Revocation of Prior Powers of Attorney. I revoke any prior health care power of attorney. The preceding sentence is not intended to revoke any general powers of attorney, some of the provisions of which may relate to health care; however, this power of attorney shall take precedence over any health care provisions in any valid general power of attorney I have not revoked.

B.   Jurisdiction, Severability, and Durability. This Health Care Power of Attorney is intended to be valid in any jurisdiction in which it is presented. The powers delegated under this power of attorney are severable, so that the invalidity of one or more powers shall not affect any others. This power of attorney shall not be affected or revoked by my incapacity or mental incompetence.

C.   Health Care Agent Not Liable. My health care agent and my health care agent's estate, heirs, successors, and assigns are hereby released and forever discharged by me, my estate, my heirs, successors, assigns, and personal representatives from all liability and from all claims or demands of all kinds arising out of my health care agent's acts or omissions, except for my health care agent's willful misconduct or gross negligence.

D.   No Civil or Criminal Liability. No act or omission of my health care agent, or of any other person, entity, institution, or facility acting in good faith in reliance on the authority of my health care agent pursuant to this Health Care Power of Attorney shall be considered suicide, nor the cause of my death for any civil or criminal purposes, nor shall it be considered unprofessional conduct or as lack of professional competence. Any person, entity, institution, or facility against whom criminal or civil liability is asserted because of conduct authorized by this Health Care Power of Attorney may interpose this document as a defense.

E.   Reimbursement. My health care agent shall be entitled to reimbursement for all reasonable expenses incurred as a result of carrying out any provision of this directive.

10. Signature of Principal

By signing here, I indicate that I am mentally alert and competent, fully informed as to the contents of this document, and understand the full import of this grant of powers to my health care agent.

This the ███ day of August, 2016.

████████████████ (SEAL)

████████████

11. Signatures of Witnesses

I hereby state that the principal, ████████████, being of sound mind, signed (or directed another to sign on the principal's behalf) the foregoing health care power of attorney in my presence, and that I am not related to the principal by blood or marriage, and I would not be entitled to any portion of the estate of the principal under any existing will or codicil of the principal or as an heir under the Intestate

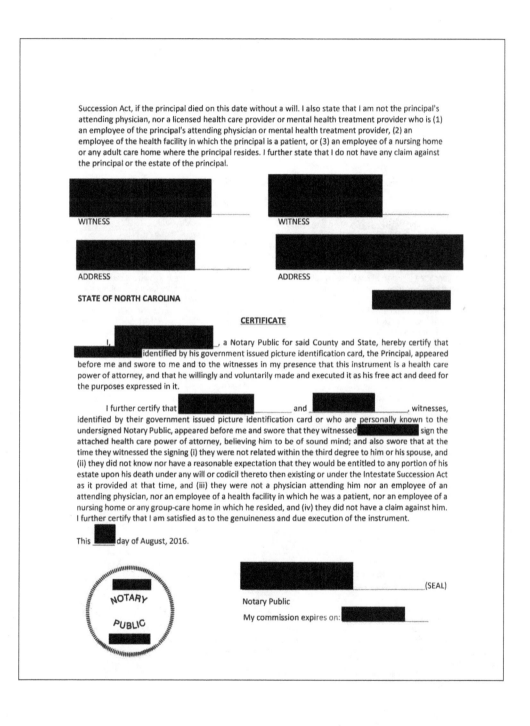

Succession Act, if the principal died on this date without a will. I also state that I am not the principal's attending physician, nor a licensed health care provider or mental health treatment provider who is (1) an employee of the principal's attending physician or mental health treatment provider, (2) an employee of the health facility in which the principal is a patient, or (3) an employee of a nursing home or any adult care home where the principal resides. I further state that I do not have any claim against the principal or the estate of the principal.

WITNESS   WITNESS

ADDRESS   ADDRESS

STATE OF NORTH CAROLINA

CERTIFICATE

I, _____, a Notary Public for said County and State, hereby certify that _____ identified by his government issued picture identification card, the Principal, appeared before me and swore to me and to the witnesses in my presence that this instrument is a health care power of attorney, and that he willingly and voluntarily made and executed it as his free act and deed for the purposes expressed in it.

I further certify that _____ and _____, witnesses, identified by their government issued picture identification card or who are personally known to the undersigned Notary Public, appeared before me and swore that they witnessed _____ sign the attached health care power of attorney, believing him to be of sound mind; and also swore that at the time they witnessed the signing (i) they were not related within the third degree to him or his spouse, and (ii) they did not know nor have a reasonable expectation that they would be entitled to any portion of his estate upon his death under any will or codicil thereto then existing or under the Intestate Succession Act as it provided at that time, and (iii) they were not a physician attending him nor an employee of an attending physician, nor an employee of a health facility in which he was a patient, nor an employee of a nursing home or any group-care home in which he resided, and (iv) they did not have a claim against him. I further certify that I am satisfied as to the genuineness and due execution of the instrument.

This _____ day of August, 2016.

NOTARY PUBLIC

_____(SEAL)
Notary Public
My commission expires on: _____

6.3.3 HIPAA Release

A HIPAA release allows your loved ones access to your medical information. (HIPAA stands for Health Insurance Portability and Accountability Act.)

Fig 6.8

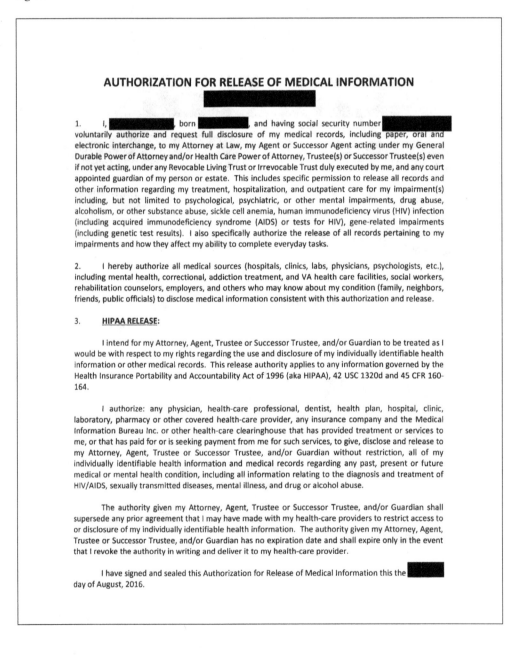

██████████████████ (SEAL)

█████████

WITNESS   WITNESS

ADDRESS   ADDRESS

NORTH CAROLINA

I, ███████████████, a Notary Public, for said County and State, do hereby certify that ████
████ being by me duly sworn and identified by his government issued picture identification card, and
███████████████ and ███████████████, witnesses
identified by government issued picture identification cards or who are personally known to the
undersigned Notary Public, personally appeared before me this day, and acknowledged the due execution
of the foregoing and annexed instrument for the purposes therein expressed.

WITNESS my hand and official seal, this ████ day of August, 2016.

████████████████ (SEAL)
Notary Public
My commission expires: ████████

NOTARY PUBLIC

6.3.4 General Durable Power of Attorney

A general durable power of attorney allows your loved ones to make business decisions for you when you can't.

Fig 6.9

Prepared by: Tovah M. Mitchell, Attorney
     Mitchell Law Group, PLLC
     P.O. Box 465
     Morrisville, NC 27560
     919-808-2405
Return to: Same

GENERAL DURABLE POWER OF ATTORNEY

ARTICLE I. **DESIGNATION OF AGENT**

Designation of Agent. I, ▮▮▮▮▮▮▮, also known as ▮▮▮▮▮▮▮ of ▮▮▮▮▮▮, North Carolina, being of sound mind, appoint my son, ▮▮▮▮▮▮ to serve as my Attorney-in-Fact (herein referred to as my "Agent") for the purposes set out below.

Designation of Successor Agent. If my Agent resigns, is declared incompetent, is not reasonably available or is unable for any reason to act as my Agent as shown by a Resignation, Order of Incompetence, or Affidavit of Unavailability by my Successor Agent, then I appoint my son, ▮▮▮▮▮▮, to serve as alternate attorney-in-fact. The successor Agent designated shall be vested with the same power and duties as if originally named as my Agent.

Appointment of Successor. If, upon the death, removal or resignation of an Attorney-in-Fact serving hereunder, no successor or surviving Attorney-in-Fact has been named herein and/or if a person named as successor Attorney-in-Fact fails or refuses to accept such appointment, the last person who served or is serving as Attorney-in-Fact hereunder who was not removed from office shall have the power to appoint a person or persons to serve as successor attorney(s)-in-fact hereunder. The appointing Attorney-in-Fact may resign and make the appointment effective immediately or the appointment may provide that it will become effective upon the subsequent death, removal or resignation of the appointing Attorney-in-Fact.

The appointment of a successor Attorney-in-Fact shall be made as follows:

  (a) The Attorney-in-Fact entitled to make the appointment shall sign and acknowledge a written instrument making the appointment;

  (b) The written instrument making the appointment shall be recorded in the office of the register of deeds where this power of attorney has been recorded; and

  (c) If the appointment was to become effective upon the occurrence of a subsequent event or condition, a written instrument signed and acknowledged by the appointee giving notice of the occurrence of such event or condition shall be recorded in the office of the register of deeds where this power of attorney has been recorded. The facts stated in the recorded appointee notice shall be conclusively presumed to be true.

ARTICLE II.   GENERAL STATEMENT OF AUTHORITY GRANTED

I grant to my Agent the power to do and perform in a fiduciary capacity as my Agent may deem advisable anything of any character which I might do or perform for myself if personally present and acting, including, but not limited to, the specific powers set forth below in Articles III, IV, and V, but excluding those matters which my Agent is not permitted to do as expressly provided in this General Power of Attorney or as provided by law.

ARTICLE III.   SPECIFIC POWERS RELATING TO PROPERTY

My Agent may exercise the following powers relating to property or interests in property, which I now own or may hereafter acquire:

Collection of Property. The power to demand, sue for or use other lawful means to obtain, collect, and take possession and control of any sums of money, debts, checks, accounts, interest, dividends, annuities, rents, goods, chattels, inheritances, insurance benefits, social security benefits, unemployment benefits, veteran's benefits and any other claims and right whatsoever which are now or may hereafter become due, owing, payable or belonging to me, and to compromise, settle, arbitrate, abandon or otherwise deal with any such claims;

Sale or Other Disposition of Property. The power to sell, exchange, quitclaim, convert, partition, grant an option on, abandon or otherwise dispose of all or any part of my real or personal property or my interest in such property, including, but not limited to automobiles, stocks, bonds, and real estate owned by me individually, as a tenant in common, tenant by the entirety or otherwise, upon any terms and conditions;

Acquisition and Retention of Investments. The power to acquire and retain for any period of time as investments, without diversification as to kind or amount, any real or personal property, or interest in such property, including an undivided, temporary or remainder interest, income or non-income producing, located within or outside the United States, and including, but not limited to, notes, U.S. Treasury Bonds redeemable at par in payment of federal estate tax, any other bonds, debentures, mortgages and other obligations, secured or unsecured, common and preferred stocks, mutual funds, legal and discretionary trust funds, general and limited partnership interests, leases and securities of any corporate Agent or any corporation owning stock of the corporate Agent or of any subsidiary or affiliate of or successor to such corporation;

Management of Property. The power to take possession, custody, control and otherwise manage any of my real or personal property, or my interest in such property, including, but not limited to, the power (i) to protect, develop, subdivide and consolidate such property, (ii) to lease such property upon any terms and conditions including options to renew or purchase for any period or periods of time and to modify, renew or extend any existing leases, (iii) to erect, repair, or make improvements to any building or other property and to remove existing structures, (iv) to establish and maintain reserves for the maintenance, protection and improvements of such property and for other purposes, (v) to initiate or continue farming, mining or timber operations on such property, (vi) to purchase and carry casualty and liability insurance, (vii) to grant or release easements with respect to such property, (viii) to dedicate or withdraw from dedication such property from public use, and (ix) to join with co-owners in exercising any such powers;

Business Interests. The power to continue to own, or to form initially, and operate any business interest, whether in the form of a proprietorship, corporation, general or limited partnership, joint venture or other organization, including, but not limited to, the power (i) to effect incorporation, dissolution or other change in the form of the organization of such business interest, (ii) to dispose of any part of such business interest or acquire the interest of

others, (iii) to continue, enter into, modify or terminate any agreements relating to any such business interest, and (iv) to invest capital or additional capital in or lend money to such business interest;

Borrowing Money. The power (i) to borrow money for my benefit from my Agent, individually, or from others, upon any terms and conditions, (ii) to secure the payment of any amount so borrowed by mortgaging, pledging or otherwise encumbering any of my real or personal property, or my interest in such property, and (iii) to modify, renew or extend the time for payment of any obligation, secured or unsecured, payable by me for any period or periods of time and upon any terms and conditions;

Lending Money. The power (i) to lend money to any person upon any terms and conditions, (ii) to modify, renew or extend the time for payment of any obligation, secured or unsecured, payable to me for any period or periods of time and upon any terms and conditions, (iii) to foreclose as an incident to the collection of any obligation, any deed of trust or other lien securing such obligation, to bid on the property at such a foreclosure sale or otherwise acquire the property without foreclosure and to retain the property so obtained;

Holding Property in Nominee Form. The power to register and hold any securities or other property in the name of a nominee or in any other form without disclosure of the agency relationship, or to hold the same in such form that they will pass by delivery;

Exercise of Security Rights. With regard to securities of mine, including stocks, bonds and any evidence of indebtedness, the power (i) to vote any such securities in person or by special, limited or general proxy at any shareholders' meeting, (ii) to consent to or participate in any contract, lease, mortgage, foreclosure, voting trust, purchase, sale or other action by any corporation, company or association, (iii) to consent to or participate in, facilitate and implement any plan of incorporation, reincorporation, reorganization, consolidation, merger, liquidation, readjustment or other similar plan with respect to any such corporation, company or association, and (iv) to exercise all options, rights and privileges, including the exercise or sale of conversion, subscription or other rights of whatever nature pertaining to any such securities and to subscribe for additional securities or other property;

Creation of Revocable or Irrevocable Trusts. The power to amend and/or to create a Revocable Trust or to create an Irrevocable Trust that provides for me alone or for me and/or my spouse, if any, and/or my descendants during my lifetime and at my death provides for my spouse, if any, and my descendants, per stirpes or is otherwise consistent with my estate plan as evidenced by my Last Will and Testament or my Living Trust, if any. Provisions for my spouse, if any, and my descendants, may include, but are not limited to, a Supplemental Needs or Special Needs Trust, as my Agent may deem appropriate. Upon my death, the trust property may be distributed in trust or outright and free of trust to my spouse and/or my descendants per stirpes, if any, or in the alternate, to those persons who would be my heirs had I died intestate owning such property;

Further, my trustee may create and fund, with so much of my income and/or assets as my Agent deems necessary or appropriate, a qualified income trust, a pooled trust or a disability trust, all as authorized pursuant to 42 USC 1396(p)(d)(4)(A)-(C) and to execute any accompanying joinder agreement for purposes of establishing a pooled trust and to nominate beneficiaries consistent with the laws governing such trust(s) and further to nominate the ultimate beneficiary, after repayment of any state or federal entity, provided such nomination is consistent with my existing estate plan, if any, and if none, then to those persons who would be my heirs had I died intestate owning such property;

Transfer of Property to and Withdrawal of Property from Trusts. The power to assign, transfer and convey all or any part of my real or personal property, or my interest in such property, to (i) any irrevocable or revocable trust established by me during my lifetime, or (ii) any irrevocable or revocable trust established by my Agent during my lifetime. The power to withdraw property from (i) any revocable trust established by me during my lifetime, or (ii) any revocable trust established by my Agent during my lifetime. The power to exchange property to and from an irrevocable trust created by me or my agent.

Gifts. The power to give any or all of my real and/or personal property, or my interest in any such property, to my spouse, to my issue and/or to the spouse of any of my issue, not necessarily in equal amounts or shares, including the power to make such gifts to my attorney-in-fact, if my attorney-in-fact is a member of the class of eligible donees as set forth hereinabove. Such power shall include but not be limited to the power to gift any or all of my property held with a bank, savings and loan, credit union, brokerage house or other institution. Such bank, savings and loan, credit union, brokerage house or other institution shall be entitled to rely on an affidavit executed by my above named attorney-in-fact stating that such transaction is authorized under this instrument. Any bank, savings and loan, credit union, brokerage house or other institution dealing in good faith with my attorney-in-fact under this instrument shall be protected and not be responsible for the misapplication of any money or other property gifted by or to such attorney-in-fact.

Any gifts made by my attorney-in-fact under this instrument must (1) be advisable for tax planning, asset protection or other purposes, specifically including but not limited to private or public benefit or medical assistance planning, and (2) be in the mutual interests of me and/or my spouse and secondarily my issue; any such determinations shall be made in the reasonable discretion of my attorney-in-fact. My attorney-in-fact shall not be limited by my history of making or joining in the making of gifts. My attorney-in-fact may continue to make gifts to religious institutions or charities that I or my spouse has historically made.

Gifts authorized by this power of attorney may be made in any manner which my attorney-in-fact deems appropriate, including but not limited to, outright gifts, gifts in trust, gifts which retain a life estate or an estate for a fixed term for me, gifts which retain a special power of appointment by me, gifts of future or contingent interests, gifts to a custodian under a uniform gifts or transfers to minors act, gifts for education given to an educational organization, or gifts for medical care given to medical services providers.

It is my desire that my attorney-in-fact attempt to maximize the impact of any present or future federal or state transfer tax (i.e., gift tax or estate tax); however, the imposition of any such tax shall not prohibit my attorney-in-fact from making gifts.

Renunciations. The power to renounce or disclaim in whole or in part the right of succession to any real or personal property or interest in such property passing to me as an heir or beneficiary under a will or otherwise when in the opinion of my Agent a renunciation or disclaimer is advisable for tax purposes.

Insurance Transactions. The power to exercise or perform any act, power, duty, right or obligation whatsoever in regard to any contract of life, accident, health, disability or liability insurance or any combination of such insurance procured by or on behalf of me prior to execution; and to procure new, different or additional contracts of insurance for me and to designate the beneficiary of any such contract of insurance, including my Agent.

Estate Transactions. The power to request, ask, demand, sue for, recover, collect, receive, and hold and possess all legacies, bequests, devises, as are owned by, or due, owing, payable, or belonging to me at the time of execution or in which I may thereafter acquire interest, to have, use, and take all lawful means and equitable and legal remedies, procedures, and writs in my name for the collection and recovery thereof, and to adjust, sell, compromise, and agree for the same, and to make execute and deliver for the principal, all endorsements, acquaintances, releases, receipts, or other sufficient discharges for the same.

ARTICLE IV.   SPECIFIC POWERS RELATING TO PERSONAL AFFAIRS

My Agent may exercise the following powers relating to personal affairs:

Support. The power to do any acts, including disbursing of any monies belonging to me, which, in the opinion of my Agent, may be necessary or proper for any purpose in connection with the support and maintenance of my spouse, my dependents and me in accordance with our customary standard of living, including, but not limited to, provisions for housing, clothing, food, transportation, recreation, education and the employing of any person whose services may be needed for such purposes.

Health Care. The power to disburse any monies belonging to me, which, in the opinion of my Agent, may be necessary or proper for any purpose in connection with my health care and the health care of my spouse and dependents, that is, any care, treatment, service or procedure to maintain, diagnose, treat, or provide for my physical or mental health or personal care and comfort and that of my spouse and dependents, including, but not limited to, the power to pay for the charges of health care providers, such as any physician, dentist, or podiatrist and any hospital, nursing or convalescent home, or other institution;

I intend for my agent to be treated as I would be with respect to my rights regarding the use and disclosure of my individually identifiable health information or other medical records. This release authority applies to any information governed by the Health Insurance Portability and Accountability Act of 1996 (aka HIPAA), 42 USC 1320d and 45 CFR 160-164;

I authorize: any physician, health-care professional, dentist, health plan, hospital, clinic, laboratory, pharmacy or other covered health-care provider, any insurance company and the Medical Information Bureau Inc. or other health-care clearinghouse that has provided treatment or services to me, or that has paid for or is seeking payment from me for such services, to give, disclose and release to my agent, without restriction, all of my individually identifiable health information and medical records regarding any past, present or future medical or mental health condition, including all information relating to the diagnosis and treatment of HIV/AIDS, sexually transmitted diseases, mental illness, and drug or alcohol abuse;

The authority given my agent shall supersede any prior agreement that I may have made with my health-care providers to restrict access to or disclosure of my individually identifiable health information. The authority given my agent has no expiration date and shall expire only in the event that I revoke the authority in writing and deliver it to my health-care provider;

Asserting My Intent to Return Home. If I ever enter a nursing home or other care facility, it is my intent to return to any home that I own or in which I have an interest. This should not limit the ability of my Agent to exercise the full powers listed in this document and I understand that there may be some circumstances where it may be best for my Agent to sell or transfer my home. I hereby authorize my Agent to execute a "Statement of Intent to Return Home" in connection with any Medicaid application or recertification that may need to be filed on my behalf.

Other Personal Affairs. The power to do acts, including the disbursing of any monies belonging to me, which, in the opinion of my Agent, may be necessary or proper in connection with the conduct of my other personal affairs, including, but not limited to, (i) continuation, use or termination of any charge or credit accounts, (ii) payments or contributions to any charitable, religious or educational organizations, (iii) dealing with my mail and representing me in any matter concerning the U.S. Postal Service, (iv) continuation or discontinuation of my membership in any club or other organization, and (v) acceptance or resignation, on my behalf, from any offices or positions which I may hold including any fiduciary positions.

ARTICLE V. MISCELLANEOUS SPECIFIC POWERS

My Agent may exercise the following miscellaneous powers:

Tax Matters. The power to perform any and all acts that I might perform with respect to any and all federal, state, local and foreign taxes, for the period between the tax years 1984 and 2084, including, but not limited to, the power (i) to make, execute and file returns, amended returns, declarations of estimated tax, joint or otherwise, and to represent me or to sign an Internal Revenue Service Form 2848 ("Power of Attorney and Declaration of Representative") or 8821 ("Tax Information Authorization"), or comparable authorization, appointing a qualified lawyer, certified public accountant or enrolled agent (including my Agent if my Agent is qualified as such a lawyer, accountant or agent) to represent me in all tax matters before any office of the Internal Revenue Service or any state, local or foreign taxing authority with respect to all types of taxes; (ii) to represent me before any office of the Internal Revenue Service or other taxing authority with respect to any audit or other tax matter involving any tax year or period, (iii) to receive from or inspect confidential information in any office of, the Internal Revenue Service or state, local or foreign tax authority, (iv) to receive, endorse, and collect checks refunding taxes, penalties or interest, (v) to execute waivers of restrictions on assessment or collection of deficiencies in tax, (vi) to execute consents extending the statutory period for assessment or collection of taxes, (vii) to execute and prosecute protests or claims for refund or applications for correction of assessed value, (viii) to execute closing agreements under IRC §7121 or comparable provisions of any state, local or foreign tax statutes or regulations, (ix) to prosecute, defend, compromise or settle any tax matter, (x) to delegate authority to or substitute another representative for anyone previously appointed by me, any Agent, or attorney, respecting any such taxes or tax matters, and (xi) to receive copies of all notices and other written communications involving my federal, state, local or foreign taxes at the home or office address of my Agent. I waive any privileges I may have against disclosure of any confidential tax information to my Agent.

If I am married, to signify, as may be required under IRC §2513 or any corresponding section of any future United States law, my consent to having one-half (1/2) of any gift(s) made by my spouse considered as made by me.

This General Durable Power of Attorney shall be deemed to apply to all types of taxes, including, but not limited to: all foreign taxes, federal income, FICA, payroll, generation skipping (and allocation of my generation skipping exemption) and gift taxes, and state and local income, payroll, intangibles, gift, and generation skipping (and allocation of my generation skipping exemption), due, reportable, or payable; and all returns to be filed on, within, or between the following years: 1984 and 2084, inclusive;

Banking Transactions. The power (i) to make deposits in or withdrawals from any account of mine in any banking, trust or investment institution, whether such account is in my name or in the joint names of myself and any other person, (ii) to open any account or interest with any such institution in my name or in the name of my Agent or in our names jointly, (iii) to endorse any checks or negotiable instruments payable to me for collection or deposit to such accounts and to sign, execute and deliver checks or drafts on such accounts, and (iv) to exercise any right, option or privilege pertaining to any account, deposit, certificate of deposit, or other interest with any such institution;

Safe Deposits. The power (i) to have access to any safe deposit box held in my name or in the joint names of myself and any other person, (ii) to lease one or more safe deposit boxes for safekeeping of my assets, and (iii) to deal with the contents of any safe deposit box, including the removal of such contents;

Individual Retirement Accounts and Qualified Retirement Plans. The power to exercise all rights, privileges, elections, and options I have with regard to any individual retirement account, pension, profit sharing, stock bonus, Keogh or other retirement plan; or other benefit or similar arrangement; including, but not limited to making withdrawals; making, changing or altering beneficiary designations, determining or amending forms of payments on behalf of me or my beneficiaries; making, changing, or altering investment decisions; changing custodians or trustees; making or completing rollovers; and making direct "trustee-to-trustee" or similar type transfers of the assets, rights, or other benefits thereof;

Social Security and Unemployment. The power to prepare, execute and file all social security, unemployment insurance and information returns required by the laws of the United States, or of any state or subdivision thereof, or of any foreign government;

Benefits from Military Service. To execute vouchers in my name for any and all allowances and reimbursements payable by the United States, or subdivision thereof, to me, arising from or based upon military service and to receive, to endorse, and to collect the proceeds of any check payable to my order drawn on the treasurer or other fiscal officer or depositary of the United States or subdivision thereof; to take possession and to order the removal and shipment, of any property of mine from any post, warehouse, depot, dock, or other place of storage or safekeeping, either governmental or private, to execute and to deliver any release, voucher, receipt, bill of lading, shipping ticket, certificate, or other instrument which the attorney-in-fact shall think to be desirable or necessary for such purpose, to prepare, to file, and to prosecute my claim to any benefit or assistance, financial, or otherwise, to which I am, or claim to be, entitled, under the provisions of any statute or regulation existing at the creation of the agency or thereafter enacted by the United States or by any state or by any subdivision thereof, or by any foreign government, which benefit or assistance arises from or is based upon military service performed prior to or after executed hereof;

Legal and Other Actions. The power to cause to be commenced, prosecuted, defended, appealed, compromised, settled, arbitrated or discontinued in my name as plaintiff or defendant, as the case may be, any legal or equitable proceedings, judicial or administrative;

Employment of Advisors. The power to employ or discharge persons, firms and corporations to advise or assist my Agent, including, but not limited to, agents, accountants, auditors, brokers, attorneys-at-law, custodians, investment counsel, rental agents, realtors, appraisers and tax specialists;

Contracting Authority. To enter into any agreement necessary or sufficient to enforce any legal right possessed by me, including but not limited to agreements pertaining to marital rights, agreements for personal services to be performed for me or on my behalf and authorizing a person, persons or agency, including my Agent, to provide personal services to me, including health care services and decisions, in exchange for a lump sum or other type of payment from my assets or income, for services rendered during my life, including the remainder of my lifetime, even if the payment depletes all of my assets or income;

Bankruptcy. To authorize the commencement of a bankruptcy case on my behalf, as provided under 11 U.S.C. § 301 (as may be amended from time to time). My attorney-in-fact may exercise this power to the same extent as any other individual debtor filing for bankruptcy relief under Chapter(s) 7, 11, 12 (if applicable), 13 and/or 15 (if applicable) of the United States Bankruptcy Code (or any other applicable Chapters or bankruptcy laws that may be added or amended from time to time). My attorney-in-fact may appear on my behalf throughout the duration of my bankruptcy case, including but not limited to at the Meeting of Creditors held pursuant to 11 U.S.C § 341 (as may be amended from time to time). My attorney-in-fact may exercise this power by authorizing the filing of any/all subsequent documents, schedules and/or related pleadings in my bankruptcy case (including but not limited to the commencement of Adversary Proceedings), and may claim any exemption(s) permitted under 11 U.S.C. § 522 and/or N.C. GEN. STAT. § 1C-1601, *et seq.* (as either or both may be amended from time to time). My attorney-in-fact is further authorized to use whatever additional powers may be needed in order to faithfully carry out on my behalf any of the duties required under 11 U.S.C. § 521 (as may be amended from time to time), or any other applicable law deemed necessary in order to carry out the process of my bankruptcy case. My attorney-in-fact is authorized to hire an attorney for the purposes of obtaining legal advice and representation when exercising the specific grant of power described in this paragraph;

Resignations and Acceptance of Positions. To resign any position which I might hold as an officer or director of a corporation, as a partner of a partnership, as a personal representative, trustee, guardian or other fiduciary or as a politically elected or appointed officer of other similar position and to accept any such position provided that my agent may only "accept" an appointment or nomination on my behalf but shall not "serve" in my stead for any such office or fiduciary position requested of me by any third party and expected by that party for me to render such service personally;

Attorney-Client Privilege. To waive the attorney-client privilege and obtain all information from any lawyer representing me or who has represented me. Any such lawyer is authorized to furnish all information requested concerning any legal representation as fully as if I had requested such information myself;

Establish Joint Survivorship Accounts and/or payable on Death Accounts. My agent may establish joint and survivorship accounts in my name and in the name of my spouse, and/or any of my children, and/or any of my grandchildren; and may establish payable on death accounts and/or transfer on death accounts wherein the designated beneficiary of said account shall be my spouse, and/or any of my children, and/or any of my grandchildren.

Change beneficiary of Life Insurance, Annuity or Retirement Accounts. My Agent may change the beneficiary of any life insurance policy or other insurance or annuity contract wherein the beneficiary of said policy shall be my spouse, and/or any of my children, and/or any of my grandchildren;

Disclaimers, Waivers and Powers of Appointment. To claim or disclaim or waive any interest in property, in whole or in part, and to exercise any power of appointment over property that I have or would otherwise receive, INCLUDING circumstances where the exercise of any of these actions would result in a benefit to my Agent, or the estate, creditors, or the creditors of the estate of my Agent, or an individual to whom my Agent owes a legal obligation of support;

Government benefits. To use the authority conferred in this Durable Power of Attorney to make decisions which my Agent may, in his or her own discretion, determine are appropriate to qualify for Medicaid or any other public benefit program and to consent on my behalf to support orders sought and obtained by my spouse for my spouse's proper support and to avoid my spouse's impoverishment; however, my Agent should exercise this power only after consultation with and guidance from a qualified Elder Law Attorney eligible to practice law in the State of my residence. I understand that my Agent may engage in such planning for such purposes as spousal protection, preservation of my assets for needs not met by public benefit programs and/or the preservation of assets for my testate or intestate or trust beneficiaries;

Retirement Accounts and Pension Plans. To apply for and receive any retirement benefit, including profit sharing, pension or other employee welfare plans and other benefits to which I may be entitled, including the right to act as my representative payee with Social Security Administration, and to exercise any right to elect benefits or payment options, and specifically including the right to terminate or withdraw from any such account or plan and to change beneficiaries of any such account or plan provided such change is consistent with my estate plan; and to change ownership of any such account or plan from me to my spouse and to consent to or waive consent in connections with the designation of beneficiaries and joint and survivor spousal rights under any such account or plan;

Life Insurance and Annuities. To purchase, sell, assign, surrender, and/or withdraw from, life insurance and annuity contracts and to exercise any and all rights of mine under such contracts including the right to designate or change owners and beneficiaries provided such designation or change of beneficiaries is consistent with the designation of beneficiaries under my existing estate plan.

ARTICLE VI.   EFFECT OF SUBSEQUENT DISABILITY OF PRINCIPAL

This General Power of Attorney is executed pursuant to Article 2 of Chapter 32A of the General Statutes of North Carolina and shall not be affected by my subsequent incapacity or mental incompetence.

ARTICLE VII.   ADMINISTRATIVE AND OTHER MISCELLANEOUS PROVISIONS

Guardianship Provision. If it becomes necessary for a court to appoint a guardian of my estate, I nominate my Agent acting under this document to be the guardian of my estate, to serve without bond or security. My agent may also serve as guardian of my person, to serve without bond or security, but my health care agent shall have priority to be appointed over my person.

Reliance of Third Parties on Agent.

1.   No person who relies in good faith upon the authority of or any representations by my Agent shall be liable to me, my estate, my heirs, successors, assigns, or personal representatives, for actions or omissions by my Agent.

2.   The powers conferred on my Agent by this document may be exercised by my Agent alone, and my Agent's signature or act under the authority granted in this document may be accepted by persons as fully authorized by me and with the same force and effect as if I were personally present, competent, and acting on my own behalf. All acts performed in good faith by my Agent pursuant to this General Power of Attorney are done with my consent and shall have the same validity and effect as if I were present and exercised the powers myself, and shall inure to the benefit of and bind me, my estate, my heirs, successors, assigns, and personal representatives. The authority of my Agent pursuant to this General Power of Attorney shall be superior to and binding upon my family, relatives, friends and others.

Revocation of General Power of Attorney. If this General Power of Attorney has not been registered in an office of the register of deeds in any county in North Carolina, then in addition to the methods of revocation provided by Section 32A-13(b) of the General Statues of North Carolina, this General Power of Attorney may be revoked by my executing and acknowledging, in the manner provided for execution of durable powers of attorney in Article 2 of Chapter 32A of the General Statues of North Carolina a subsequent General Power of Attorney, a copy of which is delivered to the Agent acting under this General Power of Attorney in person or to such person's last known address by certified or registered mail, return receipt requested.

Legal Documents and Incidental Costs. My Agent shall be entitled to sign, execute, deliver, and acknowledge any contract or other document that may be necessary, desirable, convenient, or proper in order to exercise and carry out any of the powers described in this document and to incur reasonable costs on my behalf incident to the exercise of these powers. My Agent shall have no authority to enter into any contract that mandates arbitration as a mandatory form of dispute resolution.

Duty and Limited Liability of Agent. This General Power of Attorney does not impose a duty on my Agent to exercise granted powers, but when a power is exercised, my Agent shall use due care to act in my best interests and in accordance with this document. My Agent and my Agent's estate, heirs, successors, and assigns are hereby released and forever discharged by me, my estate, my heirs, successors, and assigns and personal representatives from all liability and from all claims or demands of all kinds arising out of the acts or omissions of my Agent pursuant to this document, except for willful misconduct or gross negligence.

Accountings. My Agent shall keep full and accurate inventories and accounts of all transactions for me as my Agent. Such inventories and accounts shall be made available for inspection, upon request by me or by my guardian or personal representative. My Agent shall not be required to file any inventory or accounts with any court or clerk.

Removal and Resignation of Agent. I shall have the right to remove an Agent at any time in a writing signed by me and acknowledged before a notary public and delivered to the Agent in person or to such person's last known address by certified or registered mail, return receipt requested. An Agent shall have the right to resign in a writing signed by the Agent and acknowledged before a notary public and delivered to me and to any other Agent acting under this General Power of Attorney or, if none, to the designated successor Agent, if any, in person or to such person's last known address by certified or registered mail, return receipt requested.

Continuing Nature and Conflicts of Interest. The powers herein granted shall be deemed continuing and relate as fully to any property that I may hereafter acquire as to any property I may own, and may be exercised repeatedly.

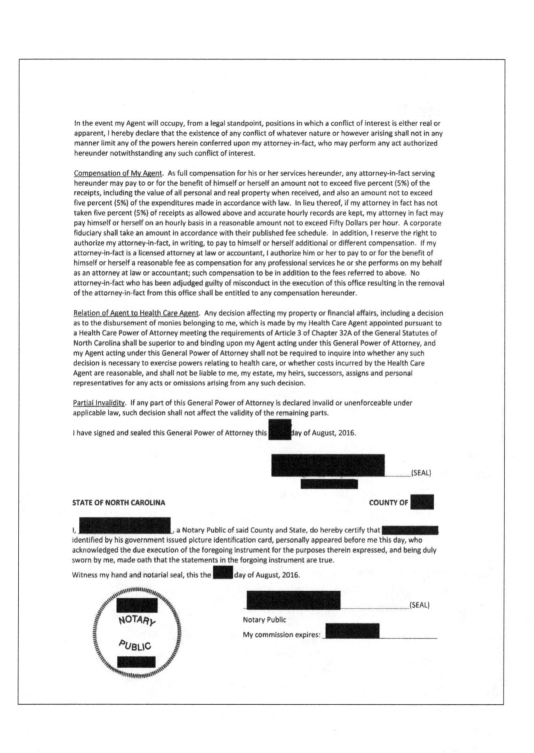

In the event my Agent will occupy, from a legal standpoint, positions in which a conflict of interest is either real or apparent, I hereby declare that the existence of any conflict of whatever nature or however arising shall not in any manner limit any of the powers herein conferred upon my attorney-in-fact, who may perform any act authorized hereunder notwithstanding any such conflict of interest.

Compensation of My Agent. As full compensation for his or her services hereunder, any attorney-in-fact serving hereunder may pay to or for the benefit of himself or herself an amount not to exceed five percent (5%) of the receipts, including the value of all personal and real property when received, and also an amount not to exceed five percent (5%) of the expenditures made in accordance with law. In lieu thereof, if my attorney in fact has not taken five percent (5%) of receipts as allowed above and accurate hourly records are kept, my attorney in fact may pay himself or herself on an hourly basis in a reasonable amount not to exceed Fifty Dollars per hour. A corporate fiduciary shall take an amount in accordance with their published fee schedule. In addition, I reserve the right to authorize my attorney-in-fact, in writing, to pay to himself or herself additional or different compensation. If my attorney-in-fact is a licensed attorney at law or accountant, I authorize him or her to pay to or for the benefit of himself or herself a reasonable fee as compensation for any professional services he or she performs on my behalf as an attorney at law or accountant; such compensation to be in addition to the fees referred to above. No attorney-in-fact who has been adjudged guilty of misconduct in the execution of this office resulting in the removal of the attorney-in-fact from this office shall be entitled to any compensation hereunder.

Relation of Agent to Health Care Agent. Any decision affecting my property or financial affairs, including a decision as to the disbursement of monies belonging to me, which is made by my Health Care Agent appointed pursuant to a Health Care Power of Attorney meeting the requirements of Article 3 of Chapter 32A of the General Statutes of North Carolina shall be superior to and binding upon my Agent acting under this General Power of Attorney, and my Agent acting under this General Power of Attorney shall not be required to inquire into whether any such decision is necessary or exercise powers relating to health care, or whether costs incurred by the Health Care Agent are reasonable, and shall not be liable to me, my estate, my heirs, successors, assigns and personal representatives for any acts or omissions arising from any such decision.

Partial Invalidity. If any part of this General Power of Attorney is declared invalid or unenforceable under applicable law, such decision shall not affect the validity of the remaining parts.

I have signed and sealed this General Power of Attorney this ▮▮▮ day of August, 2016.

_____ (SEAL)

STATE OF NORTH CAROLINA   **COUNTY OF** ▮▮▮

I, ▮▮▮▮▮▮▮▮▮▮, a Notary Public of said County and State, do hereby certify that ▮▮▮▮▮▮▮▮ identified by his government issued picture identification card, personally appeared before me this day, who acknowledged the due execution of the foregoing instrument for the purposes therein expressed, and being duly sworn by me, made oath that the statements in the forgoing instrument are true.

Witness my hand and notarial seal, this the ▮▮▮ day of August, 2016.

_____ (SEAL)

Notary Public

My commission expires: ▮▮▮▮▮▮

Reading Check

Why is it important to have your estate planning documents prepared? What are the four major documents that should be included in estate planning?

6.4 Estate Taxes

These states collect their own tax on residents' estates:

- Connecticut
- Delaware
- District of Colombia
- Hawaii
- Illinois
- Maine
- Maryland

- Massachusetts
- Minnesota
- New Jersey
- New York
- North Carolina (repealed for deaths as of January 1, 2013)
- Ohio (repealed for deaths as of January 1, 2013)

- Oregon
- Rhode Island
- Tennessee (eliminated as of January 1, 2016)
- Vermont
- Washington

Each state taxes estates that exceed a certain value. Many states exempt estates up to $1 million, but New Jersey, for example, taxes estates of $675,000 or more.

Many state tax-exemption amounts have changed in the past few years. To get the most up-to-date numbers, check the website of your state's taxing authority.

Under the step-up-in-basis-at-death rule, assets have their tax basis increased to their value on the date you pass away. This enables your beneficiaries to sell those capital assets without owing any capital gains tax, regardless of how much you initially paid for them.

For example, you purchased 50 acres of farmland several years ago for $90,000. It is currently worth $250,000. If you sold it for $250,000, you would owe capital gains taxes on $160,000. If you hold it until your death, your beneficiaries can sell the 50 acres with a stepped-up basis of $250,000, and potentially owe no tax.

Capital gains taxes for the sale of personal residences during your lifetime are exempted on gains of up to $250,000 for one person or $500,000 for a couple.

Reading Check

Does your state collect taxes on residents' estates? Where do you go to find out the details?

PREPARATION FOR LIFE INSURANCE AND ESTATE PLANNING

Life insurance policies covering me and/or spouse:

COMPANY	POLICY #	FACE AMOUNT	ANNUAL PREMIUM	BENEFICIARY(S)

I have a will ....Yes .... No

Last time updated ..../............................/.........................

KEY QUESTIONS

- Is Social Security income taxed?

- What are Medicare surcharges?

- Can you postpone income taxes?

- Are there income taxes associated with death?

- What are some long-term-care implications of income taxes?

- Can you prepare your taxes by yourself?

- Is aid available to those who need help preparing their taxes but can't afford the cost?

Corresponds to Chapter 8, "Income Taxes," in **The Complete Cardinal Guide.**

7.1 The History of the Income Tax

When the 16th Amendment to the Constitution was ratified in 1913, the income tax became a permanent feature of the US financial system. Early 1040 tax forms were one page long, including the instructions. Over the decades, as a result of political wrangling and various special-interest efforts to influence the American economy, we now have a tax code that most citizens don't understand. There are both tax breaks and tax penalties you need to learn about that impact your financial situation when you turn 65, go on Medicare, start collecting your Social Security check, start drawing down your IRA, possibly need long-term care, and pass away and leave money to your spouse or kids.

7.2 Social Security Taxes

Many people pay federal income taxes on their Social Security benefits. This usually happens only if you have other substantial income in addition to your benefits (such as wages, self-employment earnings, interest, dividends, and other taxable income that must be reported on your tax return).

No one pays federal income tax on more than 85% of his or her Social Security benefits, based on Internal Revenue Service (IRS) rules. If you:

1. **file a federal tax return as an individual and your combined income* is:**
   a. between $25,000 and $34,000, you may have to pay income tax on up to 50% of your benefits.
   b. more than $34,000, up to 85% of your benefits may be taxable.
2. **file a joint return and you and your spouse have a combined income* that is:**
   a. between $32,000 and $44,000, you may have to pay income tax on up to 50% of your benefits.
   b. more than $44,000, up to 85% of your benefits may be taxable.
3. **are married and file a separate tax return, you probably will pay taxes on your benefits.**

> **Note:*
>
>   *Your adjusted gross income*
>
> \+   *Nontaxable interest*
>
> \+   *1/2 of your Social Security benefits*
>
> =   **Your combined income**

Each January you will receive a Social Security Benefit Statement (Form SSA-1099) showing the amount of benefits you received in the previous year. You can use this Benefit Statement when you complete your federal income tax return to find out if your benefits are subject to tax.

If you do have to pay taxes on your Social Security benefits, you can make quarterly estimated payments or choose to have federal taxes withheld from your benefits.

Reading Check

If you live on Social Security and a small amount of other income, will you pay income taxes on your Social Security? If you have substantial income in addition to your Social Security, which of these is true: You will pay up to 85% of your Social Security in taxes, or up to 85% of your Social Security benefits will be taxable income?

7.3 Medicare: Income-Related Monthly Adjustment Amount (IRMAA)

The standard Medicare Part B monthly premium for 2017 is $134. If you're single and file an individual tax return, or married and file a joint tax return, the following additional costs could apply to you. While these costs are not assessed as "taxes," that's what they are in everything but name:

Fig 7.1 Medicare "Taxes," Single or Married Filing Jointly

MODIFIED ADJUSTED GROSS INCOME (MAGI)	PART B MONTHLY PREMIUM AMOUNT	PRESCRIPTION DRUG COVERAGE MONTHLY PREMIUM AMOUNT
Individuals with a MAGI of $85,000 or less Married couples with a MAGI of $170,000 or less	2017 standard premium = $134.00	Your plan premium
Individuals with a MAGI above $85,000 up to $107,000 Married couples with a MAGI above $170,000 up to $214,000	Standard premium + $53.50	Your plan premium + $13.30
Individuals with a MAGI above $107,000 up to $160,000 Married couples with a MAGI above $214,000 up to $320,000	Standard premium + $133.90	Your plan premium + $34.20
Individuals with a MAGI above $160,000 up to $214,000 Married couples with a MAGI above $320,000 up to $428,000	Standard premium + $214.30	Your plan premium + $55.20
Individuals with a MAGI above $214,000 Married couples with a MAGI above $428,000	Standard premium + $294.60	Your plan premium + $76.20

If you're married and lived with your spouse at some time during the taxable year but file a separate tax return, the following additional costs could apply to you:

Fig 7.2 Medicare "Taxes," Married Filing Separately

MODIFIED ADJUSTED GROSS INCOME (MAGI)	PART B MONTHLY PREMIUM AMOUNT	PRESCRIPTION DRUG COVERAGE MONTHLY PREMIUM AMOUNT
Individuals with a MAGI of $85,000 or less	2017 standard premium = $134.00	Your plan premium
Individuals with a MAGI above $85,000 up to $129,000	Standard premium + $214.30	Your plan premium + $55.20
Individuals with a MAGI above $129,000	Standard premium + $294.60	Your plan premium + $76.20

7.4 Roth IRA

The tax code allows you or your employer to transfer earned income into your IRA, 401(k), 403(b), and similar types of accounts, without paying income taxes or payroll taxes—*for now*. The earnings or growth inside of these accounts is tax-deferred—*for now*. Ordinary income taxes must be paid when distributions are taken from your IRA. If you distribute your IRA before age 59½, an additional 10% penalty will be applied.

With a Roth IRA, you deposit after-tax earned income. Earnings or growth accumulate tax-free inside a Roth IRA. Distributions from your Roth IRA are tax-free during your lifetime, providing you leave the money in the Roth for at least five years.

It is possible, and might be to your advantage, to convert your traditional IRA to a Roth IRA. In doing so, you pay income taxes on your traditional IRA. Roth IRAs have no Required Minimum Distributions during your lifetime. For more on IRAs, see Module 4.

Reading Check

Do you pay taxes on money in an IRA? If so, when?

7.5 How Are Different Types of Investment Income Taxed?

IRAs
Tax-deferred until withdrawn. Taxed as ordinary income.

Roth IRAs
Tax-free.

Life Insurance
Cash value increases are tax-deferred until withdrawn, then taxed as ordinary income. Death benefits generally go to beneficiaries with taxes due on deferred gains.

Stocks Held Individually
Capital gains tax is due on sale profits if the stock is held longer than 12 months. Dividends are taxed at capital gains rates.

Bonds Held Individually
Interest is taxed as ordinary income. Capital gains tax is due on sale profits if the bond is held longer than 12 months.

Bank CDs Held Individually
Interest is taxed as ordinary income.

Mutual Funds
Income tax liability is passed through to the holder of the mutual fund. It's paid as ordinary income tax or capital gains tax.

Estate Taxes: "There Are Income Taxes Even in Death"
The estate files an income tax return for the year in which the death occurred. Several considerations come into play, including "Income in respect of a decedent."

7.6 Long-Term Care and Income Taxes

Nursing home and home health-care costs can be a deductible medical expense. Generally, you can deduct only the amount of your medical and dental expenses that exceed 10% of your adjusted gross income (AGI). We believe that smart planning is to use IRA money first to pay nursing home and home health care costs.

Fig 7.3

TYPE OF TAXPAYER	PREMIUM DEDUCTION (TRADITIONAL POLICIES)		TAXATION OF BENEFITS
Individual taxpayer who itemizes deductions (Schedule A)	Treated as accident and health insurance. IRC §7702B(a)(1) Limited to lesser of actual premium paid or eligible LTCI premium. IRC §§213(d)91)9D0, 213(d)(10) Eligible LTC premium in 2017 (indexed):		**Reimbursement** benefits are not included in income. *IRC§ §104(a)(3), 7702B(a)(2)* **Per diem (or indemnity)** benefits are not included in income except amounts that exceed the <u>greater of</u>: • $360 per day (2017 indexed), <u>or</u> • Total qualified LTC expenses. IRC §§104(a)(3), 7702B(a)(2), 7702B(d)

Eligible LTC premium table:

Attained age in tax year	Deductible premium limit
Age 40 or less	$410
Age 41–50	$770
Age 51–60	$1,530
Age 61–70	$4,090
Age 71 or older	$5,110

Medicare expense deduction is allowable to extent that such expenses (including payment of Eligible LTCI premium) exceed 10% of AGI (7.5% if age 65 or older). IRC§ §213(a), 213(f)

LINKED-BENEFIT LTCI
LTC benefits paid from a Tax-Qualified (7702B) annuity or life insurance "linked benefit" plan are tax-free as noted above. *IRC§7702B(e)*
Cash surrenders from a LTCI linked-benefit plan that paid LTCI benefits may have a reduced cost-basis. *IRC§72(e)(11)*
Premium payments for annuity or life insurance linked-benefit LTCI plans are NOT deductible. (Separately-billed TQ LTCI riders may be deductible.)

7.7 Income Tax Rates

The tables below show the 2017 personal income tax rates, depending on your filing status.

Fig 7.4

Marginal Tax Rate	Taxable Income Brackets for 2017 *Ordinary* Income Tax Rates	
	Married Filing Joint	Single
39.6%*	Over $470,700	Over $418,400
35%	$416,701 – $470,700	$416,701 – $418,400
33%	$233,351 – $416,700	$191,651 – $416,700
28%	$153,101 – $233,350	$91,901 – $191,650
25%	$75,901 – $153,100	$37,951 – $91,900
15%	$18,651 – $75,900	$9,326 – $37,950
10%	$0 – $18,650	$0 – $9,325

* The top rate is effectively 43.4% for those subject to the 3.8% Medicare surtax on net investment income

Long Term Capital Gains Rate	Taxable Income Brackets for 2017 *Long Term Capital Gains and Qualified Dividends Tax*	
	Married Filing Joint	Single
20% *	Over $470,700	Over $418,400
15%**	$75,901 – $470,700	$37,951 – $418,400
0%	$0 – $75,900	$0 – $37,950

*The top rate is effectively 23.8% for those subject to the 3.8% Medicare surtax on net investment income

**Clients in the 15% LTCG tax bracket with MAGI over their 3.8% threshold ($250,000 joint filers/$200,000 single filers) will pay an effective rate of 18.8%

PLANNING FOR INCOME TAXES

Locate your prior year's tax return(s).

Your adjusted gross income (AGI) from line .... on your form 1040 =

....

MODULE 8 | **CHOOSING YOUR ADVISOR**

KEY QUESTIONS

- What is a Certified Financial Planner™ (CFP®)?

- How can you find a Certified Financial Planner™?

- Who should you buy your insurance from?

- What other professionals can a CFP® help you find?

Corresponds to Chapter 9, "Don't Try This at Home: Choosing Your Advisors,"
in The Complete Cardinal Guide.

Planning for your retirement and then living in retirement with your money requires you to have advisors with specialized knowledge and experience in the topics covered in this book. Dealing smartly with Social Security, Medicare, long-term care, IRA distributions, retirement income for life, estate planning, and income taxes all call for experts to serve the needs of senior citizens.

8.1 Finding a Certified Financial Planner™ (CFP)

Finding a financial planner specializing in senior citizens starts on the World Wide Web. One of the authors plugged in his personal profile to show you what information is available on each financial planner you search. The results are presented below. Notice that in the "specialties" area of the planner profile, you find long-term care, Social Security, retirement, estate planning, etc. These are indicators that the professional works with senior citizens.

1. Go to LetsMakeAPlan.org.
2. Click Find a CFP®PRO.
3. Enter your location to find a CFP® professional near you.

Fig 8.1

1. Go to PlannerSearch.org.
2. Enter a specific name or your location to find a CFP® in your area.

Fig 8.2

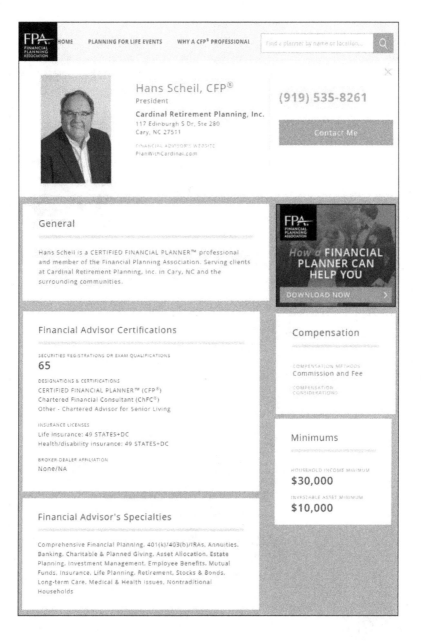

1. Go to BrokerCheck.FINRA.org.
2. Enter your current or a prospective broker's name to see their employment history, certifications, and licenses.

Fig 8.3

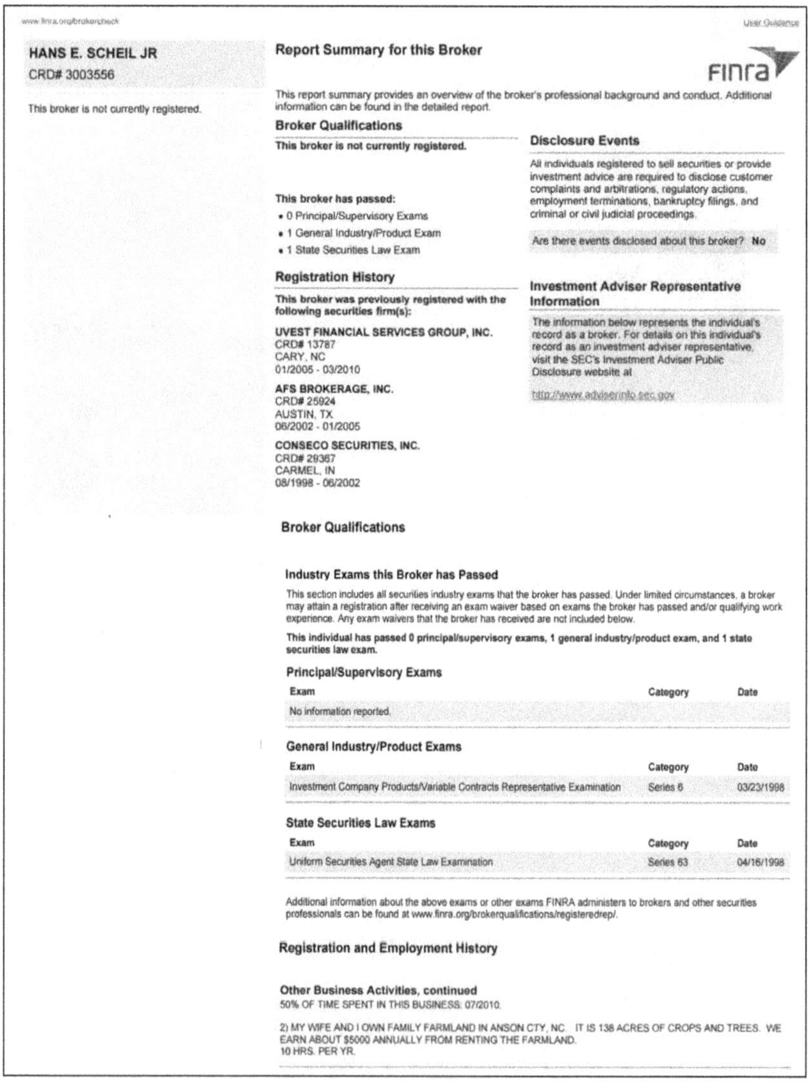
www.finra.org/brokercheck

User Guidance

HANS E. SCHEIL JR
CRD# 3003556

This broker is not currently registered.

Report Summary for this Broker

FINRA

This report summary provides an overview of the broker's professional background and conduct. Additional information can be found in the detailed report.

Broker Qualifications

This broker is not currently registered.

This broker has passed:

- 0 Principal/Supervisory Exams
- 1 General Industry/Product Exam
- 1 State Securities Law Exam

Registration History

This broker was previously registered with the following securities firm(s):

UVEST FINANCIAL SERVICES GROUP, INC.
CRD# 13787
CARY, NC
01/2005 - 03/2010

AFS BROKERAGE, INC.
CRD# 25924
AUSTIN, TX
06/2002 - 01/2005

CONSECO SECURITIES, INC.
CRD# 29367
CARMEL, IN
08/1998 - 06/2002

Disclosure Events

All individuals registered to sell securities or provide investment advice are required to disclose customer complaints and arbitrations, regulatory actions, employment terminations, bankruptcy filings, and criminal or civil judicial proceedings.

Are there events disclosed about this broker? **No**

Investment Adviser Representative Information

The information below represents the individual's record as a broker. For details on this individual's record as an investment adviser representative, visit the SEC's Investment Adviser Public Disclosure website at

http://www.adviserinfo.sec.gov

Broker Qualifications

Industry Exams this Broker has Passed

This section includes all securities industry exams that the broker has passed. Under limited circumstances, a broker may attain a registration after receiving an exam waiver based on exams the broker has passed and/or qualifying work experience. Any exam waivers that the broker has received are not included below.

This individual has passed 0 principal/supervisory exams, 1 general industry/product exam, and 1 state securities law exam.

Principal/Supervisory Exams

Exam	Category	Date
No information reported.		

General Industry/Product Exams

Exam	Category	Date
Investment Company Products/Variable Contracts Representative Examination	Series 6	03/23/1998

State Securities Law Exams

Exam	Category	Date
Uniform Securities Agent State Law Examination	Series 63	04/16/1998

Additional information about the above exams or other exams FINRA administers to brokers and other securities professionals can be found at www.finra.org/brokerqualifications/registeredrep/.

Registration and Employment History

Other Business Activities, continued
50% OF TIME SPENT IN THIS BUSINESS: 07/2010.

2) MY WIFE AND I OWN FAMILY FARMLAND IN ANSON CTY, NC. IT IS 138 ACRES OF CROPS AND TREES. WE EARN ABOUT $5000 ANNUALLY FROM RENTING THE FARMLAND.
10 HRS. PER YR.

Reading Check

Can a CFP® specialize in certain areas? How do you find this out?

8.2 Finding Other Financial Professionals

Attorneys

One of the best ways to find a list of attorneys who specialize in senior citizens is to search for attorneys with VA (Veterans Affairs) accreditation.

1. Go to http://www.va.gov/ogc/apps/accreditation/.
2. Enter a specific name or your location to find a VA-accredited attorney in your area.

Fig 8.4

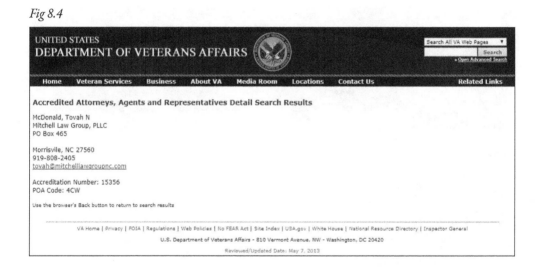

Insurance Agents

To find an insurance agent who specializes in long-term care, you can go to the CLTC® (Certification for Long-Term Care) website.

1. Go to ltc-cltc.com.
2. Click Find a CLTC®.
3. Enter a specific name or your location to find a certified designee in your area.

Fig 8.5

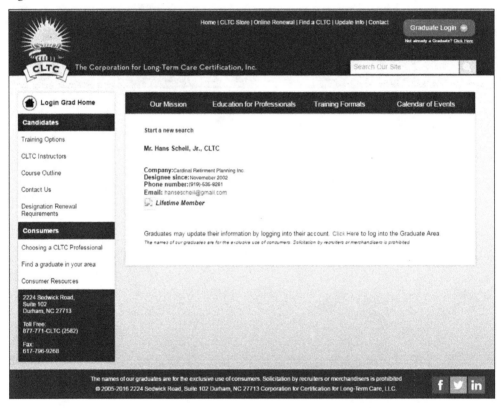

Life Insurance Professionals

To find a life insurance professional with a CLU® (Chartered Life Underwriter) designation, go to The American College of Financial Services website (theamerican-college.edu).

1. Go to designationcheck.com.
2. Enter a specific name or your location to find professionals in your area who have attained certain designations and/or advanced degrees from The American College.

Fig 8.6

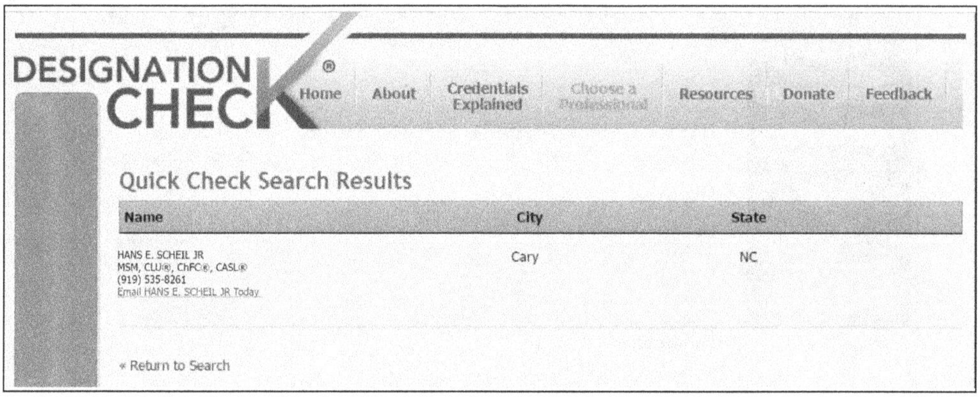

IRA Professionals

To find an IRA and qualified plan expert, go to Ed Slott's website and find one of his Master Elite Advisors.

1. Go to IRAHelp.com/find-advisor.
2. Enter your address to find an IRA advisor in your area.

Fig 8.7

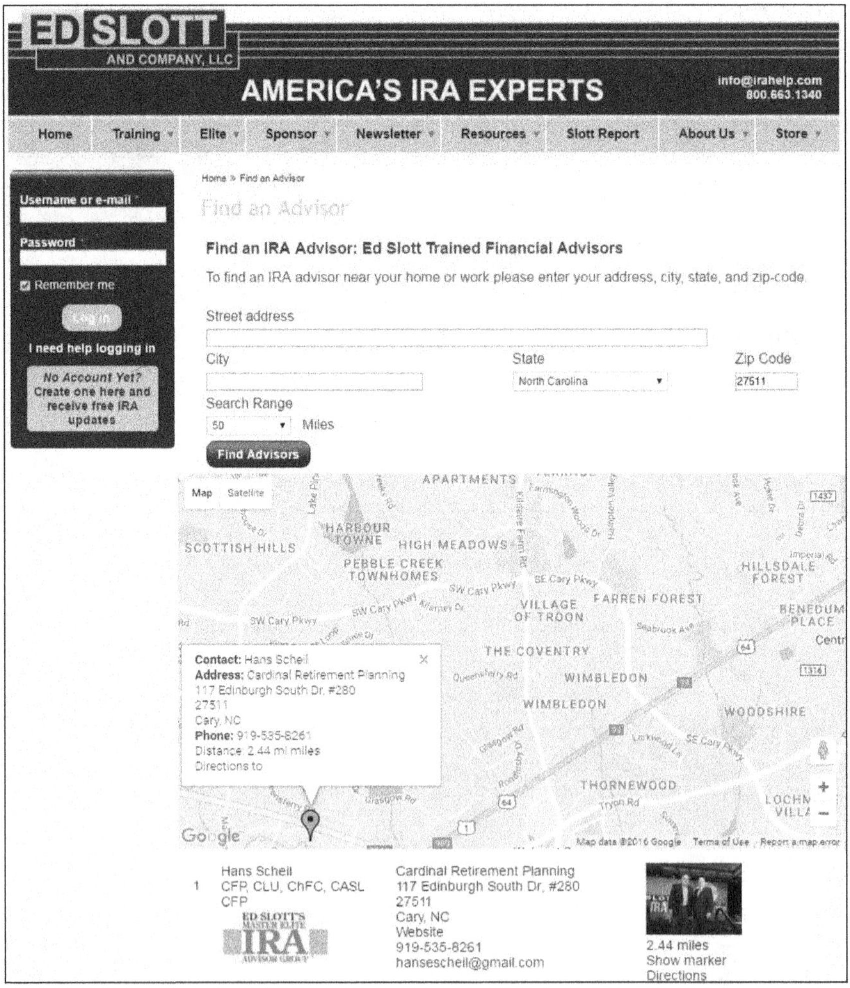

Medicare Supplement Insurance

To find an insurance agent who specializes in Medicare Supplement Insurance, go to The American Association of Medicare Supplement Insurance website.

1. Go to medicaresupp.org.
2. Click on the link to find a local Medicare supplement insurance agent.
3. Click on your state to see all the registered agents in your area.

Fig 8.8

Medicare Supplement Insurance Information

The American Association for Medicare Supplement Insurance is your source for information on this important protection. Find the most current information including Medicare supplement costs and ways to save. Request a free, no-obligation cost comparison from an Association member today.

Click Here To Find A Local Medicare Supplement Insurance Agent

American Association for Medicare Supplement Insurance
Advocacy • Information • Education • Standards

| HOME | ABOUT | CONSUMERS | CONFERENCE | INFORMATION | CONTACT US |

MEDICARE SUPPLEMENT INSURANCE (MEDIGAP) AGENT DIRECTORY

An experienced and knowledgeable Medicare Supplement insurance agent can answer your questions, can compare your options and ultimately help you apply for coverage. The agents listed below have indicated that they would like to hear from interested consumers. They will do this without any charge or obligation.

The Association always advises that you question insurance professionals about their background. Ask for references and check their reputation online (Linkedin is a good place to start). The Association takes no responsibility for the agents listed below. If you have a complaint, however, we want to hear so that we can determine if the agent no longer warrants being listed on this webpage. Call the Association at (818) 597-3205.

Jesse Slome, Executive Director, American Association for Medicare Supplement Insurance
View Jesse Slome's Linkedin Profile
Email Jesse Slome with a comment or question about Medicare Supplement Insurance
For Agents-Request information to be listed on the Association's Find An Agent Directory

North Carolina

I'm Located In Cary, NC
Name: Hans Scheil, CFP
Phone: 919-535-8261
E-mail: Email me for No Obligation Medigap Cost Information
Website: Visit Our Website

Reading Check

Besides a CFP®, what are some other professionals you might need when planning for and living in retirement?

8.3 Finalizing Your Picks

When interviewing prospective advisors, first go with your gut and ask yourself if you trust this person. Ask if they represent several insurance companies and can advise you on financial products from several different organizations. Ask if they are independent. See if they have professional designations and verify the ones they tell you about. Find out if they are a fiduciary and will be giving you fiduciary-level advice. Finally, do they specialize in senior citizens?

PREPARING TO CHOOSE YOUR ADVISOR

Cardinal services clients in all 50 states plus DC by telephone and Skype. If you have been provided with a workbook by a financial professional, please do business with that person. If you want to locate a professional trained in the disciplines covered in this book, this exercise shows you how to find one:

- Go to LetsMakeAPlan.org to find a local CFP®.

  - Read through their specialties and look for elder care, estate planning, etc.

- Go to PlannerSearch.org to find a local CFP®.

  - Read through their specialties and look for elder care, estate planning, etc.

- Go to BrokerCheck.FINRA.org to check your broker and/or brokerage firm.

- Go to www.va.gov/ogc/apps/accreditation to find a local elder law attorney.

- Go to ltc-cltc.com to find an local insurance agent educated in long-term care.

- Go to DesignationCheck.com to find a local Chartered Life Underwriter™.

  - Be sure and ask the CLU® if he or she is independent from an insurance company.

- Go to Medicaresupp.org to find a local Medicare Supplement Insurance agent.

- Go to IRAHelp.com/find-an-advisor to find a local IRA expert.

- The professionals listed here have been trained by and have access to Ed Slott, America's IRA Expert.

INDEX

ABOUT THE AUTHORS

Hans "John" Scheil is a Certified Financial Planner™ (CFP®), Chartered Financial Consultant (ChFC®), Chartered Life Underwriter (CLU®), and Chartered Advisor for Senior Living (CASL®) with 41 years of experience. He can be reached at 919-535-8261, or via email at Hans@CardinalGuide.com. See Cardinal's website at CardinalGuide.com

Douglas "Buddy" Amis is a Certified Financial Planner™ (CFP®), has Certification for Long-Term Care (CLTC®), and is a recipient of the 30 Under 30 award from The National Underwriter. He can be reached at 919-535-8261, or via email at Doug@CardinalGuide.com. See Cardinal's website at CardinalGuide.com.

CPSIA information can be obtained
at www.ICGtesting.com
Printed in the USA
FSHW012320110122

9 781946 507013